CAREERS
IN MEDICINE

TERENCE J. SACKS

VGM Career Horizons
a division of *NTC Publishing Group*
Lincolnwood, Illinois USA

Cover photo courtesy of the Rehabilitation Institute of Chicago.

Library of Congress Cataloging-in-Publication Data

Sacks, Terence J.
    Careers in medicine / Terence J. Sacks — 2nd ed.
        p.   cm. — (VGM professional careers series)
    Includes bibliographical references.
    ISBN 0-8442-4448-1 (hbk. : alk. paper). — ISBN 0-8442-4449-X
(pbk. : alk. paper)
    1. Medicine-Vocational guidance.   I. Title.   II. Series.
R690.S23   1997
610.69—dc20

96-26670
CIP

Published by VGM Career Horizons, a division of NTC Publishing Group
4255 West Touhy Avenue
Lincolnwood (Chicago), Illinois 60646-1975, U.S.A.
© 1997 by NTC Publishing Group. All rights reserved.
No part of this book may be reproduced, stored in a retrieval
system, or transmitted in any form or by any means,
electronic, mechanical, photocopying, or otherwise,
without the prior permission of NTC Publishing Group.
Manufactured in the United States of America.

6 7 8 9 0 VP 0 9 8 7 6 5 4 3 2 1

CONTENTS

ABOUT THE AUTHOR

Terry Sacks is an independent writer-editor with more than 25 years' experience in communications. During that period he has written dozens of news stories, magazine articles, and speeches. Sacks's articles have appeared in such publications as *Hospitals* and *Chicago Medicine*.

Sacks, a graduate of Northwestern University's Medill School of Journalism, has strong credentials in the field of healthcare. For three years, from 1970 through 1973, he was director of communications for the Chicago Medical Society, the local professional group for physicians in Chicago and Cook County. He has also held positions in communications for the American Osteopathic Association, the American Association of Dental Schools, and for several hospitals in Chicago.

Sacks is currently on the journalism faculty of Columbia College in Chicago, where he teaches "Introduction to the Mass Media." At Columbia he has also taught courses in news reporting, feature writing, editing company publications, and the history of journalism.

For the past ten years, Sacks has headed his own writing and communications firm, Terence J. Sacks Associates. He is active in the Independent Writers of Chicago (where he is also on the board), the American Medical Writers Association, and the Publicity Club of Chicago.

His daughter, Lili, an internist who practices in Seattle, Washington, has been most helpful in the completion of this manuscript.

FOREWORD

Medicine. It is the story of our attempts to treat and prevent disease. Its heroes are (or should be) well known: Hippocrates, Jenner, Pasteur, the Curies, Jonas Salk. For every pioneer in the medical profession, there are many physicians, nurses, and other care providers who help us overcome illness, whether it be a common cold or a more complex disease.

The most high profile of these care givers is the *primary care physician*. In our culture it is the physician who most often delivers babies, diagnoses and treats illnesses, writes prescriptions, and attends to our health concerns. The physician—and his or her place in the medical profession—is the focus of his book.

Careers in Medicine presents a short history of medicine and describes the challenges facing the modern physician. It offers practical information about getting into medical school, financing your education, choosing a specialty, and dealing with the rigors of a medical education. More particularly, it offers a balanced discussion of the approaches to treatment taken by those in two branches of the profession: medical doctors and doctors of osteopathic medicine. The appendixes offer a list of U.S. and Canadian medical schools and medical organizations and specialty boards, plus suggestions for further readings about careers in medicine.

In the coming decade physicians will face the challenges of caring for an aging population in our society, using increasingly complex diagnostic and surgical tools, and researching cures and treatments for diseases such as AIDS.

If you are interested in playing an active role in medicine's continuing story, *Careers in Medicine* may help you decide what part you'd like to play.

The Editors
VGM Career Books

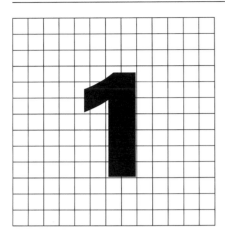

A LOOK AT THE PROFESSION

SORTING THROUGH FACT AND FICTION

So, you want to become a doctor. Perhaps you've seen such exciting and dramatic shows on TV as *Chicago Hope* and *ER* and you'd like to be a part of the action.

You've seen the main protagonists of these shows try to move heaven and earth to revive a young university professor in the last stages of life who has tried to kill himself or a young child who has been brought nearly dead into the emergency room after being struck by a hit and run driver.

But wait . . . this is TV. Real life isn't that way. Even if you wind up working in the emergency room, it is highly doubtful that you will run into any of the heartbreaking and emotion-draining situations depicted on TV. Go into any emergency room today, even those trauma centers attached to large university-operated hospitals, and chances are you will find a waiting room filled with mothers of young children varying in age from infant to two years in various stages of respiratory disease—children with hacking coughs or high fevers, or children who have been throwing up. Or perhaps you will see elderly citizens who are gasping for oxygen or experiencing sudden weakness or stomach upset.

Sure, if you were working in one of the large university hospital emergency rooms, you might run into victims of stabbings, gang fights, or auto accidents, but even here, such cases are in the minority. The truth is that most cases that come into the emergency room are not even emergencies. People come there because, for a variety of reasons, they have nowhere else to go: they have no doctor, their doctor is out of town, they have no hospitalization insurance, or they may be unable to pay for the visit and they know that they will not be turned away in the emergency room.

**Medicine's
Many Challenges**

To be sure, medicine, even the more routine and humdrum type of medicine outlined above, does have its compensations. For one, the pay is good. According to the AMA (American Medical Association), medicine's primary professional organization, doctors today average about $189,000 a year. Other medical practitioners do considerably better, such as surgeons averaging $267,000, radiologists $259,000, and anesthesiologists, $224,000 a year, according to the AMA. And these are just averages—there are many surgeons, anesthesiologists, and radiologists whose salaries are probably double those figures.

Then, too, you are on the cutting edge of technology. If you are a surgeon, you may be involved in bypass surgery in which veins taken from a patient's legs are grafted to the arteries leading to the heart to replace damaged or clogged blood vessels. Or you may do angiography, a diagnostic procedure where a thin tube called a catheter is fished through a patient's arteries and into the heart to give doctors a good idea of where the artery is blocked and what the extent of the blockage is. There are also countless new medications, such as antibiotics to stem the ravages of disease, medicines to keep cholesterol from clogging the arteries, or medicines to lower the effects of high blood pressure, to name but a few. Yes, medicine can be very exciting and challenging as you use all of this new technology, drugs, and equipment to cope with disease and illness. But that's just one side of the story.

Medicine can also be a real downer. If you don't believe it, just talk to family doctors, internists, general practitioners, whomever. Ask them and they'll tell you what it's like to be jolted from a sound sleep by a mother whose infant has a high temperature at 2:00 AM, or by the patient who imagines that he is having a heart attack at 4:00 AM when he is simply suffering from the results of having eaten too much rich food the night before.

And your doctor will tell you of the frustrations of medicine in dealing with the federal government, insurance companies, and other health payers looking over his or her shoulder or patients waiting to sue for the slightest hang-up. On the one hand, he or she is prevented from ordering certain tests needed to confirm a diagnosis, because this is not part of the rules. On the other hand, he or she faces costly and perhaps ruinous lawsuits for malpractice if the patient can prove a doctor did not pursue certain tests that might have been called for to arrive at a particular diagnosis. This is just a small idea or some of the frustrations that doctors often feel.

Then there are the long hours. Doctors' hours are long—let there be no misunderstanding about that; they work about sixty hours a week. Sure, the pay is good, but when you figure the length of time it takes to become a doctor—about eleven years counting four years of college, four years of medical school, and three years of residency, at least—and the fact that it is extremely difficult to get into medical school—you need to be in the top 10 percent of your class academically—as well as the expense of paying for a medical education, it presents a different picture. (It costs about $22,000 per year in tuition and fees alone to attend medical school today, according to the most recent figures of the Association of American Medical Colleges.) You can see why we say that becoming a doctor—and staying one—is no picnic. But if you are persistent and still believe that medicine is for you, read on.

Case Study

We'll start with a more or less typical situation involving a patient whom we will call Casey Johnson. Casey's medical problems began when during a visit to San Francisco he experienced chest pains while climbing some of the hills for which the city is justly famous. Right there Casey knew that something was radically wrong, but he had not realized just how bad the situation was until he had discussed his problems with his internist. After examining Casey's electrocardiogram, the internist referred him to a cardiologist, a heart specialist, at a large university-connected hospital. There the cardiologist had Casey undergo angiography. During this procedure, the cardiologist inserted a thin catheter (plastic tube) into Casey's groin where it then passed through the aorta and into the heart cavity. A dye was then inserted to help doctors view the heart, its chambers, and the arteries so that they could determine the precise nature and location of the blockage. Sure enough, the X-ray film taken during the procedure had revealed severe blockage of three of the arteries leading to Casey's heart. Stressing the severity of the situation, Casey's cardiologist urged that he have bypass surgery as soon as possible to correct the problem, and Casey was scheduled for surgery the following Tuesday morning. That morning the surgeon, dressed in surgical green, dominated the operating room with its bright lighting dome and the tilting operating table that positioned the patient exactly as the surgeon wanted. Assisting was the nursing staff, ranging from those who slipped on the surgeon's gown and gloves to the head surgical nurse who stood ready at the operating table, anticipating his every move. The residents, doctors in training for their speciality—cardiovascular (heart) surgery—watched intently as the surgeon worked over the inert patient. Earlier the anesthesiologist, poised over a battery of monitoring equipment, had injected Casey with a powerful anesthetic. In a matter of minutes, Casey, a businessman in his mid-fifties, had lost consciousness. Now, as he lay on the table oblivious to all that was happening, the anesthesiologist was monitoring all of his vital signs—pulse beat, blood pressure, breathing— to make sure that all was going as it should.

Earlier the surgeon had begun the procedure by cutting through Casey's breastbone (sternum) to gain access to the heart cavity. Now, thanks to an ingenious and highly complex machine, the surgeon had treated Casey with a combination of bypass surgery and a new procedure called transmyocardial laser revascularization. This new procedure was being tested at the medical center as part of a national study, in which the surgeon, using a laser, "drilled" holes about the size of a pencil into the heart muscle. For patients such as Casey with advanced coronary artery disease, the procedure offers relief from pain. In Casey's situation it was combined with bypass surgery to get him back on the track to good health. While the surgeon performed his critical work, the heart-lung machine took over the entire function of the heart and lungs. Plastic tubes carried blood from the body to the heart-lung machine, which then warmed or cooled the blood, removed carbon dioxide, added oxygen, filtered it, and then pumped the blood back to the body. Afterwards, the machine was disconnected and the revived heart and lungs resumed their normal functioning. Altogether the procedure would last four and a half hours, one of several such procedures the hospital had scheduled that day and one of an estimated twenty-six million operations performed in the United States every year.

We have cited this case in detail because it illustrates the complexity and intensity of modern medicine as performed at major medical centers all over the United States and Canada by leading practitioners. Already we have met the surgeon, the head of the team, who is responsible for the intricacies of heart surgery. Also in on the procedure was a highly skilled team of assistants made up of nurses, surgical residents, and the anesthesiologist. The latter, as we have seen, got Casey ready for surgery by injecting him with an anesthetic that put him "out" for the length of the operation. He then monitored Casey's vital signs to make sure that he remained under and felt no pain during the operation. Contributing greatly to the success of the entire procedure was Casey's cardiologist, who had diagnosed his condition after ordering the angiogram and other vital heart tests. Following surgery, the cardiologist worked with Casey's internist (personal physician) to devise a treatment plan to enhance Casey's complete recovery. This plan included medication, diet, exercise, and other factors.

Also involved at various stages of the case were other specialists. A radiologist worked with the cardiologist to study the X-ray film during the angiogram and judge the extent of the blockage. A pathologist worked with a large group of technicians, who in this case would run a series of tests on Casey's blood samples, which were obtained at various stages of his hospitalization. The tests in turn would reveal such things as cholesterol, triglycerides, hemoglobin, and red and white cells, all of which help physicians determine the relative health or illness of the patient.

Thus we see that a bypass operation, one of thousands such procedures performed yearly in the United States and Canada, calls on the services of an array of medical specialists who are supported by technicians, nurses, and medical residents. To some degree, Casey's surgery is typical of the procedures performed in the hospital, though perhaps not all are as complex or involved.

RANGE OF THE PROFESSION

Today doctors, or physicians, as they are more accurately known, handle a variety of functions and procedures at the hospital and at various other settings: offices, surgicenters and freestanding emergency rooms, clinics, long-term care facilities (primarily nursing homes), psychiatric and rehabilitation hospitals, and many other places.

The procedures performed and the skills involved vary considerably from one specialty to another. Thus while the anesthesiologist, the pathologist, and the radiologist preside over an array of very complex equipment, they have little, if any, contact with patients. Internists and other primary care physicians, such as general practitioners, pediatricians, and obstetrician-gynecologists, have almost constant contact with patients from the time the patients enter the office until they are admitted to the hospital for tests or surgery and through their subsequent discharge and convalescence.

Medicine's Two Branches

Where various medical specialists work and the jobs they handle vary quite widely. In 1994, according to the Bureau of Labor Statistics, physicians held approximately 560,000 jobs. This included both M.D.'s (medical doctors) and D.O.'s (doctors of osteopathic medicine). In 1994 there are approximately 37,000 osteopathic physicians in the United States. They were concentrated primarily in Florida, Pennsylvania, Michigan, Texas, New Jersey, Ohio, and Missouri.

Although these two branches of medicine—M.D.'s and D.O.'s—are fairly similar in their approach, there is one primary difference. Doctors of osteopathy stress the musculoskeletal system and often include spinal manipulation in their treatment as a means of getting all of the body systems into harmony.

But individual doctors in both branches are licensed to prescribe medications, deliver babies, perform surgery, and admit patients to hospitals. For years the two branches went their own ways and had their own superstructures. Osteopathy had its own medical schools, state and local organizations, specialty certifying boards, and even its own hospitals. But in recent years, while the two branches maintain to some extent their own superstructure, the differences between the two are blurring as doctors of osteopathy are being admitted to M.D.-dominated hospitals and medical societies.

So, to a great extent, what is said in the rest of this book about M.D.'s pertains to D.O.'s as well. And the book will point out those instances where the two branches diverge.

Where Doctors Work

In 1992 two-thirds of all doctors' practices were office based, including clinics and HMOs; 20 percent worked out of hospitals, holding such specialty jobs as anesthesiologist, radiologist, pathologist, neonatologist (specializing in newborns), and emergency room physician.

Others are involved in a wide range of jobs, such as working for an HMO (Health Maintenance Organization), emergency medicine clinic, surgicenter, and so forth. Still others work in the public health area for state or local health departments in public health medicine. Others are involved in aerospace medicine or handle research, primarily patient oriented, at medical centers across the United States and Canada. Some doctors combine teaching at large medical schools with research, and perhaps maintain private practices as well. A few serve as administrators of HMOs, group practices, nursing homes, hospices, and a variety of other health enterprises. Yet others work for private companies or industries where, among other duties, they test and examine employees and review their medical records. So, as you can see, the field is vast and there is plenty of room for persons with a variety of skills and interests.

A PROFESSION IN FLUX

But today medicine is a profession beset by powerful forces, many of which it is powerless to control. These include rapidly escalating costs that have far outstripped other components of the cost of living index; radical and far-reaching discoveries in the treatment and diagnosis of disease; a seeming avalanche of government and third-party payer restrictions to help cap runaway costs; and changing attitudes on the part of consumers as to the profession and to individual doctors. All of these forces have impacted the profession, many of them negatively from the viewpoint of the individual physician.

Take for instance the way consumers feel about individual doctors and the profession as a whole. Several surveys by the AMA and others have shown that although people think highly of their own physicians, they often think negatively about the profession as a whole. For instance, one recent survey showed that 63 percent of those polled thought that doctors were too interested in making money and only 42 percent believed that doctors explained adequately, if at all, the options available to patients.

As a result of this largely negative view of doctors, the AMA launched a $1.75 million campaign several years ago to uplift the public's views of physicians. It took out a series of ads in such publications as *Time*, *Newsweek*, and *U.S. News* to achieve this goal. Whether it succeeded is still doubtful at this point.

Indicative of how the profession's image has eroded is the upsurge in malpractice suits. According to John Dwight and Edward J. Dwyer in their book *The American Almanac of Jobs and Salaries*, there were 20,000 such suits in the early 1990s. Such escalation of the number of malpractice suits meant a corresponding increase in the cost of malpractice insurance for the individual doctor; according to the AMA this cost approached $15,000 per physician in 1993.

For years doctors were looked up to as respected members of the community. In recent years, however, this image has been widely eroded, as consumers fed up with out-of-sight increases in health care have vented a part of their anger on the profession and on other health care providers, such as hospitals and nursing homes.

From 1970–74 the number of applicants per medical school spot was 2.8. By 1988 this figure had dropped to 1.6. However, by 1994–95 medical school applicants per spot rebounded to 2.6, close to the same figure as that of the mid-1970s, with women now comprising 42 percent of the applicants, compared with only 11 percent in 1970. Despite this sharp increase in the number of applicants to medical school, the chances are still pretty good that you will be accepted—about a 38 percent chance overall.

Despite this somewhat mixed picture, the fact remains that while medicine is in many respects a very satisfying profession, there are some problem areas that you should be aware of.

Negative Aspects

For one, the medical school curriculum is rough, and it isn't getting any easier. The proliferation of information in the areas of medical technology and treatment has created what at times seems an impossible mountain of facts to be assimilated. This is particularly true during the first two years, referred to as the basic science years, where in most schools students are subjected to a barrage of statistics and facts on subject matter that they are asked to retain throughout medical school, indeed throughout their careers in medicine. Under such circumstances, it becomes not so much a matter of what you can digest, but what you can learn by rote, and students with a photographic memory are at a tremendous advantage over their classmates. Because of this emphasis on rote learning, which often seems miles removed from the clinical practice of medicine, schools have been experimenting in recent years with making the first two years of medical school more relevant to the practice of medicine.

Another cause of much grief and controversy arises from the rigors of residency training (the years medical students, now doctors, devote to learning their specialty or subspecialty). Residents average a workweek in many cases of nearly eighty hours and are on call every third or fourth day for twenty-four hours at a time. Not only does this result in sleep deprivation and lack of alertness by the residents, but it often means inferior treatment for patients, too. Hospitals and other training institutions are well aware of the problem and are taking steps to make the hours and the working conditions of residents more humane.

Compounding the problem is the worry of working mothers who are torn between their duties to their patients and to their children. In many cases such working medical moms, especially during the years of their residency training, suffer pangs of guilt as they must surrender time at home to their work schedules.

There are several other problem areas that confront doctors once they establish their practices, especially if they are in one of the primary care areas of medicine, such as pediatrics, obstetrics, geriatrics, family practice, or internal medicine. Doctors in these areas of practice will soon learn what it is to have a patient take a turn for the worse after working for perhaps months on helping the patient to recover from an illness. Often, despite the physician's best efforts, the patient may weaken and die, leaving the physician to ask: Where did I go wrong? What else might I have done to help keep my patient alive?

Then the doctor also must deal with all sorts of patients. Calls from patients come in at all times, day and night. Some calls are justified; some are not. Many patients are kind and considerate to be sure, but sickness makes others ill tempered, and often they tend to blame their doctor for their problems, especially if there is little that he or she can do.

Add to this the hours, which are lengthy and irregular. According to the Bureau of Labor Statistics, nearly half of all doctors worked a sixty-hour workweek in 1994, although nearly a fourth worked a more normal forty-hour workweek.

To these concerns pile on the problems of unpredictable and hostile patients, the physician's declining image, the ever-mounting problems of malpractice—a never-ending source of worry and expense—and the ever-increasing bureaucracy the physician faces in dealing with government red tape and that of other third-party payers, and you can see why so many physicians face burnout and early retirement. Indeed, it has been estimated that one in thirty-one doctor deaths in the United States result from suicide, while the figure for the nation as a whole is one in seventy deaths.

Positive Aspects

Although all of these problems are cause for concern, they are hardly the entire picture by any means. There are many positive aspects of medicine that make it all worthwhile and one of the most gratifying professions of all. To a large extent these positive aspects more than compensate for all of the negatives listed above.

For one there is the endless variety of the work. As one resident put it: "You have to be on your toes . . . human beings don't behave like machines . . . every encounter is different . . . a new challenge."

And the relationship between doctor and patient can be extremely gratifying. Most patients look up to their doctor and regard him or her with respect, if not affection, even as they are concerned with health care costs and their health in general.

In all truth many patients, if not most, want to take part more fully in decisions about their health. Depending on the physician's viewpoint, he or she can consider this a chance to educate the patient, or as a bothersome annoyance. To most physicians, however, this is an opportunity to help patients learn new and more constructive ways of living as far as diet, exercise, sleep, and medication are concerned—changes that can profoundly affect their patients' lives.

As noted above, the profession has been undergoing tremendous change. Not the least of these changes is the tremendous explosion in new treatments and therapies, drugs, and lifesaving methods that were not even dreamt of say thirty or forty years ago.

Take the marvels of bypass surgery. Here many men and women seriously ill from the damage caused by hardening of the arteries and poor blood circulation have been offered new hope and a chance to lead more normal lives. Forty-five years ago such a procedure was not even on the drawing board let alone available. Think of all of the lives that could have been saved had such bypass surgery been around at the time.

Or consider all of the experimentation in artificial hearts, heart and other organ transplants, laser surgery (commonly used in many hospital procedures, particularly in diabetic retinopathy), and microsurgery to help eliminate the ravages of disk problems in the spinal cord and in hip and knee replacement, and you get some idea of how far the profession has come in recent years.

Now look at the gigantic strides the profession has made in the area of disease diagnosis. Take for instance angiography, in which the heart and the arteries are opened up to the most probing and definitive of diagnoses yet; and then there are the fields of computerized tomography (CT) scans, magnetic resonance imaging (MRI), ultrasound, nuclear medicine, and other testing procedures that help doctors get a better and more realistic picture of disease and its effect on the patient.

From this you can get some idea of the progress that medicine has made in recent years. As one physician put it: "When I was a resident, back in the late sixties, we had perhaps a choice of four medications to control hypertension (high blood pressure). Today we have . . . perhaps a hundred medications for this, and seemingly there are ten medications to control hypertension coming out every few months." All of this progress makes it almost impossible for the physician to keep up-to-date on disease, yet another cause for physician insecurity.

With new drugs and therapies being announced almost every day, medicine is in a state of ferment. What's true today will almost certainly be old hat in ten years. This means that the conscientious physician must spend a lifetime of study trying to keep abreast of what is going on in the field.

Compensation

But most doctors are handsomely compensated for their efforts. A recent AMA study revealed that income for all doctors reached an all-time high in 1993 of $189,000. This was a jump of more than 100 percent over the $89,000 that physicians were averaging in 1981.

Surgeons had the highest earnings of all specialties, averaging $262,700 a year. Twenty-five percent of all surgeons earned $150,000 or less per year while another 25 percent earned $320,000 per year. It should be noted that these figures are after all expenses, but before taxes.

On the lower end of the scale, family physicians earned the least, averaging $116,000 a year. Twenty-five percent earned less than $75,000 and a quarter earned more than $149,000 a year.

These are just averages. It seems safe to say that many physicians earn $350,000 to $600,000 and more annually, especially well-known surgeons, anesthesiologists, and radiologists in large hospitals.

Physician earnings, according to the Bureau of Labor Statistics, were higher than salaries paid to other professionals. The BLS reported that in 1993 averages of the highest levels in the professions were more than $134,000 for lawyers, $76,000 for chief accountants, $102,500 for engineers, and $105,000 for personnel directors.

Even so, according to Dr. C. John Tupper, 1991 president of the AMA and a former medical school dean from Sacramento, California, "Physicians deserve good pay because they devote about twelve years to higher education, spend fifty-five to sixty hours a week on the job, and experience high stress." He adds that, "some workers get time and a half for overtime and night differential. Physicians don't."

Costs

Though the pay is excellent, this is somewhat offset by the cost of education. According to the Association of American Medical Schools, tuition in 1995 averaged $22,873 per year. It was considerably less for public schools, averaging $8,760 for residents and $19,362 for nonresidents.

Small wonder why one medical school dean observed that more than half of all medical school graduates are finishing school more than $50,000 in debt and as many as 5 to 6 percent are finishing with debts of more than $100,000. Add to this the fact that tuition in most universities is increasing at a rate far outstripping that of inflation, and we have a problem of enormous dimensions.

Still another concern of almost undreamt of proportions in recent years is that of malpractice—particularly as it affects those in the most vulnerable category—obstetrics (physicians involved in the delivery of babies). According to the AMA, average professional liability insurance (malpractice) premiums paid by employed physicians rose from $10,500 in 1985 to $14,400 in 1993, an increase of almost 4 percent annually.

As a result, says the AMA, for this period (1985 to 1993) nearly 8 percent of a physician's income went to pay higher premiums for malpractice insurance. So the cost of malpractice insurance is very much a factor in rising health care costs, particularly so in the case of obstetrician-gynecologists, who in 1993 paid the highest rates of all doctors for malpractice insurance premiums—an estimated $33,700 a year.

So there it is, some of the positives and negatives of a medical career, with no attempt to gloss over the negatives affecting the profession or to give the positives an undue sheen.

A LOOK AT WHAT'S TO COME

The chapters to come will delve further into some of the factors involved in considering medicine as a career. Chapter 2 will trace the growth and development of the profession from earliest recorded history to the present.

Chapter 3 will look at what is involved in choosing a medical school and will discuss the medical school curriculum. This chapter will also review medical school exams and their importance in obtaining residencies and in licensure and will explore postgraduate training in the various medical specialties and subspecialties.

Chapter 4 will review what is involved in paying for a medical education, aid available from the schools themselves, from government, and from other private sources.

Chapter 5 will look at what is involved in choosing a medical specialty and will examine current procedures in obtaining a residency in that specialty. Chapter 6 will examine the other branch of medicine—osteopathy. Chapter 7 will look at various options open to you in getting started, such as working as a salaried employee, starting your own practice, being a part of a group practice, or joining an HMO or other managed medicine program.

Chapter 8 will discuss the future of medicine. Chapter 9 will examine what various members of the profession—medical school administrators, teachers and researchers, students, residents, and practicing physicians—have to say about the profession, both good and bad. Finally, Chapter 10 will describe the various specialties and subspecialties available to the student who is interested in a medical career.

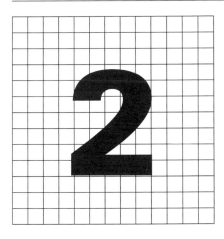

MEDICINE FROM THE DAWN OF CIVILIZATION

Although people have always been preoccupied with problems of health and well-being, it has not been until the last 200 years that most of the major discoveries in the science of medicine have been made. And since the work of Edward Jenner, an English physician who in 1796 performed the first small-pox vaccination, the pace of medical discovery and technology has been accelerating. Today one reads nearly daily of new medications and new medical procedures and technology in the treatment of disease that were undreamt of just few decades ago.

HISTORY OF MEDICINE

But even in ancient times, people were concerned with questions concerning health care and treatment. To be sure much of this care was associated with magic, superstition, and religion, and to a certain extent this is still true in certain cultures.

As a result, medicine often did more harm than good, even in relatively modern days. For example, disease was by far the major killer in the Civil War, claiming two of every three mortalities during the fighting. Scurvy, dysentery, typhoid, diphtheria, and pneumonia accounted for many thousands of deaths. In one year, 995 of every 1,000 soldiers in the Union Army contracted diarrhea and dysentery. Sanitary conditions were primitive or nonexistent.

The practice of medicine was a real concern of ancient rulers. Perhaps the first known example of such concern is found in the Code of Hammurabi of Babylon, dating back to 1727 B.C. It states: "If a physician operates on a free-man and causes the man's death or blindness, the physician's hand will be cut off." The code also stated that if the death of a slave resulted from the physician's care, the physician would have to pay for a replacement.

Hippocrates

In many ways the foundation of modern medicine can be traced to ancient Greece to a physician named Hippocrates, whose name today is synonymous with the highest standards of medical ethics. Although Hippocrates may not have been directly involved in any medical remedies, he did establish an approach to medicine that has served as one of the pillars of the profession down through the centuries. Hippocrates and his associates established the principles of the scientific method as they observed their patients. From their observations they drew conclusions as to the cause and treatment of the disease.

Hippocrates is further credited with developing the code of medical ethics that is still a foundation of modern medical practice. It says in part: "I will practice my profession with conscience and dignity; the health of my patient will be my first consideration." Today all physicians in this country swear to uphold this code of conduct when they take the Hippocratic oath.

Aside from the contributions of Hippocrates, the medical efforts of the ancient Greeks took the form primarily of disease prevention through diet and exercise.

From the Roman Empire to the Renaissance

The rise of the Roman Empire witnessed a steady decline in the recording of medical information. It remained for the Arabs and Jews to take on the job of gathering medical information; but the Romans did contribute great advancements in sanitation and the use of water aqueducts at the height of their power. Unfortunately the fall of the Roman Empire witnessed the destruction of the canals and waterways the Romans had built.

The connection of medicine to the welfare of mankind was first recognized by the Holy Roman Emperor Frederick II, who in 1240 A.D. postulated: "The damage and suffering that occur to our subjects is due to the ignorance of physicians and must be remedied." His solution was to enact a series of regulations requiring all medical practitioners to receive a diploma from a university following three years of study and a year of apprenticeship under an experienced physician. In addition, surgeons were required to take a course in anatomy. In effect, Frederick's actions formed the prototype of medical education that has guided the study of medicine down through the centuries.

The Renaissance of the fourteenth through the sixteenth centuries witnessed a revival of new inquiry and emphasis on the scientific method. Universities began to teach anatomy and physiology, and medical training became more thorough. Preeminent in the development of medical science of the era was the work of Vesalius, a Belgian physician who in 1543 published the first text on anatomy, thus distinguishing the *science* of medicine from the *practice* of medicine.

Later, in the seventeenth century, came the work of the Italian scientist, Galileo Galilei, who first used the compound microscope to observe the human body. Galilei's work was followed by an Italian physician, Giovanni Battista Morgagni, who published the first book on pathology, basing some of his observations on the primitive autopsies of the period.

But it was not until the mid-eighteenth century that anyone was able to link disease with existing unsanitary conditions and filth. And still another hundred years would elapse before scientific researchers finally understood that it was organisms attacking the body that caused disease and infection.

THE BEGINNINGS OF MODERN MEDICINE

In 1796 Edward Jenner's groundbreaking work in developing the first smallpox vaccination helped to bring this scourge under control. And it was Louis Pasteur, a brilliant French chemist, who discovered the process of using heat to control germs in milk—a process that is known today as pasteurization.

Several other developments in the nineteenth century had a profound impact on the development of medicine. First there was the work of Robert Koch, a German scientist working with Pasteur, who identified specific organisms that cause several diseases. Today he is known as the father of bacteriology, and for his efforts he was awarded the Nobel prize in physiology and medicine in 1905.

A Hungarian physician, Ignacz Semmelweis, is recognized as the pioneer of antiseptic practices in obstetrics and for his work in diagnosing blood poisoning as the cause of disease taking the lives of new mothers. And an American dentist, William Thomas Green Morton, is credited with the development of the modern science of anesthesiology, when in 1846 he first demonstrated the effectiveness of ether as an anesthetic. Morton's discoveries opened up the field of medicine to a variety of surgical operations that until then were often too painful for patients to withstand.

Using the newly acquired knowledge of the role of germs in causing disease, an English physician, Joseph Lister, introduced the concept of antisepsis in controlling and eradicating disease. He was also responsible for introducing aseptic conditions, which emphasized complete cleanliness to help keep wounds free of germs.

In 1895 William Conrad Roentgen, a German physicist, pioneered his historic work in demonstrating how a beam of electrical current passed through the body could reveal internal body structure. His discovery of what has come to be known as the X-ray enabled physicians to see inside the body, a task that until then could only be done by surgery or autopsy.

Since the turn of the century, there have been several important developments in the treatment of disease, starting with the efforts of Pierre and Marie Curie, who discovered radium, a weapon that could be used to fight cancer.

Another important step forward in medical science was the discovery of sulfa drugs by German scientist Gerhardt Domagk. Thanks to this discovery, doctors could now treat such diseases as meningitis, blood poisoning, and venereal disease.

Another important weapon in the arsenal against disease was gained with the discovery of penicillin, the first of the antibiotics, by a Scottish bacteriologist, Alexander Fleming.

A few years later physiologist Howard W. Florey showed that penicillin could fight infectious diseases. Then, in 1949, bacteriologist John Enders isolated the polio virus, thus paving the way for the development of the first effective vaccine against polio by Jonas Salk in 1954. Yet another leap forward was made with the contributions of Albert Sabin, developer of the first important oral vaccine against polio.

In more recent years scientists have crossed the threshold of new frontiers of genetic research. The most ambitious genetic study to date is a $3 billion, fifteen-year project funded by the National Institutes of Health to map all 100,000 of the genes that comprise a human being. Such research, scientists believe, can offer clues and solutions to a variety of problems, from cancer to birth defects.

In addition medical science in recent years has witnessed new treatments and surgical techniques such as cryosurgery, surgery performed with the use of special instruments that freeze human tissue; open heart surgery, including heart bypass operations; microsurgery, which uses the microscope and employs minute surgical instruments for delicate surgery; and the use of laser in surgery, especially in diseases of the eyes.

Public Health

Although medicine has made dramatic advances in recent years in the care, treatment, and diagnosis of disease that result in an improved life expectancy for all of us, this has come about not only because of medical science, but because of the impact of the public health movement as well. This movement started in the United States in the mid-nineteenth century.

Unlike personal health care, which concentrates on the care and treatment of the individual, public health focuses on the broad sweep of issues that impact the general population. In past years, for example, public health services set up the quarantine and isolation of disease-carrying animals and individuals. Other efforts to halt the spread of disease involved inoculation of the population, cleaning of streets and the draining of swamps, and the purification of drinking water, among others.

In addition, mass vaccination and public education steps were undertaken to combat disease. Largely as a result of the success of these programs, such diseases as cholera, typhus, typhoid fever, and yellow fever have been largely eradicated.

Today the work of public health agencies is being continued through the efforts of such agencies as the Center for Disease Control and the World Health Organization. These agencies strive to improve public health through large-scale public relations and education programs designed to make people more aware of the dangers of such health hazards as smoking, alcohol and drug abuse, and environmental pollution.

Public health agencies also have assumed responsibility for keeping vital statistics on births, illnesses, and deaths. Such statistics are useful in measuring the level of health in Canada and the United States and in comparing it with that of other nations. Such figures also provide important information in discovering public health problems, such as tainted meat and canned goods, and in undertaking programs to control them.

Largely due to the rapidly advancing body of medical knowledge in the treatment, diagnosis, and prevention of disease, the medical education process has become more complex.

RECENT DEVELOPMENTS IN THE MEDICAL FIELD

Changes in Education

Prior to the twentieth century, a part of every physician's training in the United States and Canada included serving an apprenticeship with an experienced M.D. Today physician training involves not only years of formal study, but postgraduate training referred to as a *residency*. Today all doctors must have their professional degree—either M.D. or D.O.—practical training, and licensure to practice medicine. They also must be certified by a specialty board and pass special certifying examinations before they can be classified as a specialist.

Changes in the Nature of the Profession

Not only has medicine witnessed the widespread advances described above, but the very nature of medicine has changed drastically as well.

Morris Abram, a well-known attorney and patient advocate who chaired the President's Commission for the Study of Problems in Medicine, put it this way: ". . . prior to 1935, doctors were therapeutic nihilists. They did not intervene unless there was something specific that they could do. Most just sat around and waited until the crisis passed."

Despite the comparatively small arsenal of medical weapons at a doctor's disposal, Abram observes that interestingly enough, there was no such thing as malpractice. "There was a lot of laying on of hands rather than the laying of hands on machinery," he notes.

According to James Sammons, formerly executive vice president of the American Medical Society, medicine until the fifties and sixties was almost solely male and predominantly fee for service. "The patient was responsible for payment of services, and insurance coverage was a plus." Partnerships, group practices, and medical clinics, not to say managed health care, were few and far between or nonexistent. "They were all outside the traditional mode of practice," Sammons observes.

But this has all changed drastically, Sammons says. Excluding residents in training and doctors who work for the federal government, one of four physicians is employed by someone else—another doctor, a corporation, a group, a hospital, or some other body. Dr. Sammons notes that AMA studies show that today of all doctors thirty-six years old and under, 46 percent of the women and 47 percent of the men are "on someone else's payroll."

Furthermore, according to the AMA, more than 77 percent of all physicians are engaged in some kind of managed care—Health Maintenance Organizations (HMOs), Independent Practice Arrangements (IPAs), or Preferred Provider Organizations (PPOs). This is considerably higher than the 42 percent of all physicians who contracted for such services in 1986. Another estimated 13 percent of all physicians devoted part or all of their practices to ambulatory care centers, emergency centers, family care, or other specialty care centers.

Nor is the profession any longer all male. AMA studies show that women presently comprise 20 percent of all physicians. What's more, about 41 percent of all medical school entrants are women, according to the Association of American Medical Colleges.

Doctors today are no longer primarily generalists. Until the start of World War I, medicine was primarily the domain of the general practitioner. In those horse and buggy days the doctor, who often rode miles in the middle of the night to set a bone or care for a tiny youngster with a high fever, was a figure of respect, even awe. Doctors could be depended upon to come no matter what the hour or the weather conditions to be faced. Honored staff members of any hospital they cared to join, they usually had no trouble getting a hospital appointment, taking care of charity work on the wards, and visiting their own hospitalized patients.

As late as the 1950s, an estimated 80 percent of all practicing physicians were general practitioners (GPs). Today it is just the opposite. General practitioners, now more commonly referred to as family practitioners, account for only about 10 percent of all physicians; the rest are specialists of one kind or another.

Specialization

In part this is due to the vast increase of medical knowledge and techniques that has so profoundly impacted the profession in the last forty or fifty years. Specialization is also where the higher salaries happen to be, although this is changing as shall be seen in Chapter 10. Another reason for the movement to ever-increasing specialization is the fact that doctors must try to acquire as much information as they possibly can. But the fund of medical knowledge is so vast that it is impossible for any one doctor to know it all. It is still quite possible, however, for individuals to become quite knowledgeable in their particular specialty or subspecialty.

There has to some degree been a resurgence of interest in general or family medicine after a long period of decline. During this period the number of general practitioners reached an all-time low of 44,000 of the total physician complement. Today, however, family medicine is the second most popular choice of specialties among medical students—next to internal medicine.

Family Medicine

There are some very good reasons for this comparative upsurge in interest in general or family medicine. First, there is an acute shortage of primary care physicians of whom the family practitioner is foremost. Second, the government, medical schools, and all facets of the profession have been promoting family medicine as an all encompassing part of medicine, in which the physician treats, diagnoses, and works on disease prevention for all patients. Then, too, many medical students have been turned off by what they regard as the trend toward mechanization, or dehumanization, of the profession, which they believe is the result of specialization. Others prefer to live and practice in rural areas, away from the larger cities.

Finally, there is the variety and challenge associated with all medicine, but particularly with family medicine. As one practitioner put it: "No two days are alike. First you have an obstetrics case, then a paraplegic, followed by an elderly patient with diabetes and arthritis. There is no end to the variety of patients you see. You never know what is going to come into the office next."

Despite this increased interest in family practice, there is no denying that most students finishing medical school today will enter one of the more than twenty-four specialties and sixty-six subspecialties of medicine. These will be described in full in Chapter 10.

CHANGES IN THE PRACTICE OF MEDICINE

Home Health Care

If the profession has changed radically in the kinds of practitioners that there are—that is, from the generalist to the specialist—so has the kind of medicine being practiced. Consider that the average doctor today, unlike the practitioner of yesterday, finds house calls wasteful and self-defeating. Studies have shown that in the time required to make one house call, half a dozen patients can be seen in the doctor's office.

Also, the equipment required to diagnose and treat patients is almost always lacking in the home. So what is the invalid or bedridden patient to do? In some communities physicians willing to make house calls have joined together to service bedridden patients.

Complicating the picture is the fact that in the next ten years, nearly one in every three patients will be over age sixty-five. This will almost certainly increase the need for home care.

Then, too, hospitals are under pressure by the federal government and third-party payers (primarily insurance companies) to release patients more quickly in an effort to cut costs. Longer recovery periods following discharge almost certainly means even more need for home health care.

Although much of this load can be assumed by nurses, nutritionists, and other health care workers, physicians will be needed increasingly to check patient medical progress as they recover.

Heavy Patient Loads

The patient load per doctor has also reached new heights with workweeks of sixty hours or greater reported currently for more than half of all physicians, especially those in primary care. This includes all internists, family physicians, pediatricians, and obstetrician-gynecologists—often the first physicians patients are likely to see.

Fueling this trend toward heavier work loads for most doctors are several factors. The rise in population and in life expectancy means that more and more patients need care. Patients are living longer because medical advancements have eradicated such former scourges as polio and tuberculosis. And as people live longer, the incidence of such chronic conditions as arthritis, diabetes, heart disease, and so forth, all increase, and accordingly, this increases the need for more physicians.

Also, the trend toward ever-greater reliance on private insurance companies and the federal government to pay for health care has encouraged many who previously might have done without it because of the cost to seek health care. At present it is estimated that more than 50 percent of all doctor and hospital bills are paid by private insurance. Fifty years ago patients themselves paid nearly 90 percent of all health and medical expenses.

People today are exposed to more health information and data on new advances in medicine through the media—newspapers, magazines, radio, and TV—which has made the population more likely than ever to seek medical treatment. The widespread distribution of public health messages through the media has also played a part in drumming up public interest in health care.

Partly as a result of this ever-increasing demand for doctors, medical schools during the 1970s launched an effort to graduate more doctors. In recent years, however, this trend has abated considerably, and many foresee a surplus of physicians in the future, especially in certain specialties, if the supply of new graduates continues at the present rate.

Where Patients Are Treated

Another factor complicating medicine today is the number of options available to doctors in treating patients. Formerly physicians were limited to seeing patients in their offices or visiting them in their homes. Today, however, physicians have almost an unlimited array of choices as to where they can see and treat patients. A few of the more commonly used options are listed below.

Hospitals.   This is where doctors have almost from the start in this country sent patients who required hospitalization.

But today, besides admitting patients to the hospital, doctors can in almost all hospitals arrange to see patients in a variety of settings, such as outpatient clinics for treating such areas as obstetrics, pediatrics, orthopedics, skin disorders, gastrointestinal problems, and ophthalmology.

The variety of services offered by physicians on an outpatient basis has expanded to include such things as hernia repair, breast biopsy, cataract surgery, tonsil removal, and many other conditions. Even those hospitals not offering such outpatient services regularly will provide outpatient care in their emergency room.

The advantage to patients is that they can often be treated at lower cost than if they were hospitalized. Also, they can spend any recovery time required in a cheerier atmosphere than that of the hospital.

To the physician such outpatient services means they can have all of the hospital's personnel and facilities—such as laboratory, X-ray, nuclear medicine, physical medicine, and rehabilitation—close at hand and in a more convenient setting.

Emergicenters.   Today a good many doctors find employment working in emergicenters, often called surgicenters, a rather recent arrival on the medical scene. Here patients with emergency problems can be treated at almost any time (some are open twenty-four hours a day). The kind of treatment received is like that received in the hospital emergency room, except that there is no hospital attached. And many of these cases could just as easily be handled in the doctor's office, except for the greater convenience such centers offer by being open longer hours than the doctors' offices. Such freestanding emergency centers offer care on a drop-in basis without appointment, like the hospital, but at considerable lower cost and usually without the long waits associated with hospital emergency rooms.

Nursing homes.   Formerly regarded as the "last stop" where patients went to spend their remaining days, nursing homes now function primarily as temporary stopping off places where patients recovering from such crippling and disabling injuries as stroke, hip fracture, or other illness can regain their strength. Quite often elderly patients, those sixty-five to eighty and older, stay only until they are strong enough to return to independent living.

Most nursing homes offer care and monitoring for those requiring assistance in such daily chores as eating, dressing, bathing, or going to the toilet. Long-term skilled care and medical attention are available in some homes.

Hospices.   These are facilities where the so-called terminally ill or dying patients and their families receive care. The idea behind the hospice movement is that patients in the terminal stages of life should spend their remaining time in as comfortable a setting as possible.

The hospice staff tries to remove the two biggest fears of the terminally ill—fear of pain and of being alone. Pain relief is given as appropriate, while the staff provides complete nursing care and reassurance. During the patient's last days, the staff makes sure that the patient is not alone.

After death the hospice often seeks to counsel the family during their bereavement.

Other treatment facilities.   There are many other facilities where physicians can and do admit patients, depending on their disability. For patients suffering from stroke or crippling or disabling injury involving their feet or arms, there are rehabilitation hospitals. There such patients can receive the care and treatment that they require.

There are also mental health facilities for patients undergoing mental stress or suffering from long-term mental illness. Birthing centers provide mothers with a place to have their babies in comfort.

MANAGED HEALTH CARE

In recent years the *managed health care* facility has come into prominence. Often referred to as *cookbook medicine* by some doctors, managed care refers to the effort of some groups that pay for health care to control costs by prescribing the types of treatment allowed. For example, such groups might restrict the type and number of tests that a physician can order, based on the patient's diagnosis or symptoms. They might also limit the number of days a patient can be hospitalized for a given diagnosis.

Included in the category of managed care are such providers as Health Maintenance Organizations (HMOs), Preferred Provider Organizations (PPOs), and Individual Practice Arrangements (IPAs). All three are sources of employment and medical practices.

HMOs are an alternative to traditional health care coverages that provide comprehensive coverage for the subscriber. For a given amount, paid in advance, the subscriber is covered for preventive physical examinations, which aim at preventing medical problems from becoming serious. The subscriber is also covered for more serious medical problems that are usually included in conventional health care plans as well.

HMOs are literally sweeping the country. According to the AMA, HMO enrollment grew by almost 6 million or 13.1 percent in 1994, up from an already high 9.7 percent growth rate in 1993. Some medical experts figure that HMOs would be serving 100 million members by the year 2,000, a tremendous achievement for an industry that had only 12.5 million enrollees as recently as 1983.

An estimated 77 percent of all physicians participated in some form of managed care plan in 1994, 55 percent in HMOs alone. PPOs are a network of physicians designated by a given insurance company to provide medical services. In joining the network, the physician-member, as well as hospital members and other health care providers, agree to accept a lower fee for services than the going rate. In exchange the doctor is assured of a definite number of patients.

Some insurance companies offer special inducements to consumers to use a physician in the PPO. For example, a carrier may offer to pay the full cost of health care rather than just a given percentage, or the carrier may waive the deductible.

GROUP PRACTICE

Unlike the doctor practicing around the turn of the century, today's practitioner prefers to practice in a group rather than as a solo practitioner. There are several reasons for this, not the least of which are the economies to be attained by forming such a group. There are many fixed, overhead expenses such as rent and electricity, which are much more economical for a group practice than for a solo practitioner. Also by pooling their funds, group members pay much less per individual for furnishings and equipment than a solo doctor would have to in outfitting an office or waiting room. Also doctors practicing in a group can cover for each other when they are away or on vacation. By splitting on-call schedules for the weekend, doctors are able to enjoy most weekends for themselves or with their families.

In a group practice there is also more likely to be an office manager or some clerical worker designated to handle the seemingly endless paperwork required by the government and other third-party payers in processing claims. These are but a few of the reasons for the rise in popularity of the group practice—a trend that is expected to continue and to accelerate, at least for the near future.

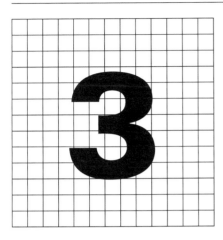

APPLYING TO MEDICAL SCHOOL

Are you right for medical school? Do you have what it takes to succeed in medicine? These are important questions whose answers you must be sure of before you apply to medical school.

Why? Because medicine is a lifetime commitment. You must study constantly to keep up with what is happening, and even then you will be lucky if you can keep up with just what is occurring in your specialty.

PERSONAL AND ACADEMIC COMMITMENTS

Bear in mind that it requires ten to thirteen years of higher education to become a physician: four years of undergraduate study, four years of medical study, and from two to five years of residency, depending upon the specialty that you choose. That's a substantial chunk of your life. True, some medical schools—thirty in all—offer combined undergraduate and medical programs in an effort to accelerate the completion of the entire study program in only six or seven years. But this is a very limited program that enables only a few exceptionally well-qualified high school seniors to participate. One school—the University of Missouri-Kansas City—has tailored the curriculum, including undergraduate college and medical school, to a six-year period by having it extend right through the year, with no time off for vacations. And other schools are now offering combined college-medicine degrees as well.

Although residency training (required if you want to specialize) is not a must to complete medical school, nearly every medical school graduate does opt for specialization. Only about 2 percent of the roughly 16,000 graduates in 1995 elected not to choose a residency, and these were primarily students who intended to concentrate on research or pursue another degree.

For nearly all medical students, residency training is yet another hurdle they must clear in their quest for a medical career—which means yet more years of study.

Grade Point Average

Still another very important obstacle in choosing a medical career, besides the long-term commitment to study, is the fact that medical school is very demanding, calling for a real willingness to study and to put in the time required, especially during the first two years.

If your high school grade point average is less than 3.0 or a B average, you will have a hard time getting into medical school. Consider that the mean average of students admitted during 1994 was 3.46. Of those admitted, about 53 percent had a grade point average of 3.5 on a 4.0 scale. This does not mean that you won't get in with a grade point average of less than 3.0—medical school admissions committees do allow for illness, financial problems, need to work, and other extenuating factors in reviewing qualifications of medical school applicants; but you will have to demonstrate strong leadership ability and improved academic performance, especially in your last year or two of college.

Motivation

In considering the pros and cons of a medical career, you should also bear in mind the long hours involved in completing a residency. Currently this involves an eighty-hour workweek and the need to be on call every third or fourth day. On call means that you are expected to be at your work station, ready for duty for twenty-four hours at the very least, and perhaps as long as thirty-six hours at a crack. This is indeed a powerful work commitment. Are you up to fulfilling the demands of such a workweek?

And while you're at it, ask yourself if you are truly dedicated to serving the needs of your fellow human beings. Are you willing to work with your patients on the closest of terms after they have suffered a long and debilitating illness? Are you willing to do whatever it takes to help nurture them back to health? Do you enjoy working with people of all walks of life and from varying backgrounds? Do you have the emotional stability to cope with the stress of seeing a patient die?

If you are unsure of your answers to these questions or uncertain of your ability to do the work, you would do well to reconsider a medical career, or at the very least explore the field further before reaching a final decision. You might, for instance, obtain a summer job in a hospital in your community as an orderly, working with patients or transporting them to various departments in the hospital. Any job that will put you into close contact with patients—all kinds of patients—with varying degrees of illness will help to give you an idea of what is involved in working with them. You might also get a nonpaying job as a volunteer—again perhaps transporting patients about the hospital, delivering their mail, or handling various other odd jobs in the hospital setting.

Besides grade point average and motivation, there are other requirements that you must meet to get into medical school.

Other Requirements

First, while all schools recognize the importance of a broad education, all seek a strong background in the sciences (biology, chemistry, physics, and mathematics), solid communications skills, knowledge of computers, and strong credentials in the humanities and the social sciences.

Specifically, medical schools require a year of biology, two years of chemistry (including organic chemistry), and a year of physics. Additional science courses are not required, nor are they even recommended. Breadth of educational background is the key.

Math courses, while not strictly required, are strongly recommended, including college math and calculus. And increasingly schools are also looking for computer theory and statistics in your college background. Also strongly encouraged are honors courses and independent study or research.

Although most schools require at least three years of undergraduate work, it is a fact that 89 percent of the students admitted have their bachelor's degree, 6 percent, their master's degree, and 2 percent have their doctoral degree.

Note that a science major, over and above the courses listed above, is not required for medical school. A science major will not necessarily increase your chances for acceptance. The Association of American Medical Colleges, for example, has found that students majoring in the humanities did just as well or better than those majoring in the sciences.

The MCAT

One thing further that you would do well to prepare for is the MCAT (Medical College Admission Test). This standardized test is required for admission by 120 of the 125 medical schools in the United States and for admission to the Canadian schools as well. It tests applicants for medical school in four general areas: verbal reasoning, physical sciences, writing ability, and biological sciences. In 1991, in response to rapid changes in medical education and practice, the test was revised to encourage students to expand their studies to include the natural and social sciences and the humanities.

Although the test is offered twice yearly, in the spring and fall, schools prefer that you take the test in the spring approximately eighteen months before you graduate. The test, which runs a total of $5^{3}/_{4}$ hours, is administered and scored by the American College Testing program (ACT). A manual describing the content and skills evaluated is available at most college bookstores, or it can be obtained directly from ACT (see listing in Appendix B).

Also available from ACT is a registration packet listing announcements, a registration card and current information on dates, test locations, and other basic information on the test. It should also be available from your health professions adviser.

Although the $150 fee for taking the test is sizable, a fee reduction program lowering the cost of the exam to $55 for students pleading financial hardship is offered by the Association of American Medical Colleges.

It should be noted that taking this test at the time prescribed is very important. Medical school admissions committees rely heavily on the test results in deciding on your suitability for admission. Payment of the registration fee entitles you to have the results sent to any six schools of your choice. Additional copies can be sent to any other school to which you are applying for a slight additional fee.

As has already been stated, the MCAT is but one of the factors that schools consider in evaluating your credentials. Besides your grade point average and transcripts, which also are closely reviewed, most schools require a personal essay, the main points of which are described below.

Also very important are letters of recommendation from your instructors and college advisers attesting to your academic ability and your personal qualifications.

The last step in the admissions process, and a very important one, is a personal interview at any of the schools in which you are interested. This is also discussed below.

APPLYING TO MEDICAL SCHOOL

After evaluating your suitability for a medical career, both as to personal traits and academic skills, there remains the question: To which school or schools do you apply? We say schools, because most medical school applicants apply to an average of twelve schools each.

At this point, let's put to rest some of the horror stories that crop up about how tough it is to get into medical school. Certainly it is not easy, make no mistake about that, but it is not out of the realm of possibility if you can meet the very tough requirements outlined above. For example, you may have heard of one prestigious Ivy League school that received 4,200 applications for 120 openings. While this may sound impossible, it's not as bad as you may think. It does not mean that your chances for acceptance are one in thirty-five, for this does not take into account the fact that today's student applies on the average to twelve medical schools. On this basis, then, the 4,200 applications translates to only 350 bona fide applications, which brings your chances for acceptance at this particular school to one in approximately 3, or 33 percent.

Actually your chances for acceptance are just about that. Of the 45,365 students filing applications in 1994, 16,287, or 36 percent, were accepted; slightly better than one of three applications were accepted.

Of these applicants, 41.9 percent were women and the balance men. In addition, there were 5,060 underrepresented minority applicants, including African Americans, Mexican Americans, mainland Puerto Ricans, and native Americans. Of these 2,173 (42.9 percent) were accepted.

So, it comes to this: If you can meet the steep academic and personal requirements, your chances of being accepted in medical school are pretty good.

The question still remaining: To which medical schools should you apply? There are 124 American medical schools and an additional 16 in Canada. How do you select the one best suited for you?

Here are several questions that you should ask yourself to help decide the issue:

1. Do you prefer a small or a large school? Generally speaking, the state-supported public schools have more students and larger lecture classes. Smaller, private schools have a better ratio in number of faculty per student, which could be a factor in how well you learn.

2. Do you prefer classes in which lectures are stressed, or smaller classes where more personal contact between students and instructor is nurtured? While the smaller classes may offer more opportunities for close contact, you may prefer the larger class group for any of several reasons, including the opportunity it offers for working together with your classmates in study groups.

3. Are you interested in research, in clinical practice, or in teaching medicine? Which schools are known to excel in these areas? Certain of the prestigious schools, such as Cornell, Harvard, and the University of Chicago, are known to graduate large complements of students who go into research or teaching. The University of Chicago's Pritzker School of Medicine, for instance, turns out the greatest percentage of students (estimated at 20 percent) who go into research or teaching.

   Graduates of other schools, such as the University of Illinois, excel in the clinical practice of medicine—for example ophthalmology, ENT (ear, nose, and throat), and public health medicine. Check with your college academic health adviser. He or she may be of great assistance in helping to identify schools that excel in certain disciplines.

4. Where do you want to practice and what kind of medicine do you wish to pursue? If you would like to practice in a rural area, for example, it would hardly pay to apply to one of the more prestigious, competitive schools. You would probably be better off at one of the state-supported public schools.

5. What are your needs for financial assistance? Make no mistake about it—medical school is very expensive. The 1994-95 tuition rates for students entering medical school were as follows:

Private schools.   Ranged from $14,788 to $22,914 with average tuition and fees at $22,874.

Public schools.   Ranged from $2,564 to $15,138 with average tuition and fees at $8,760 for residents, and $19,362 for nonresidents.

Don't let financial need deter you from picking the very best medical schools you can find. Often the small private school may offer a better financial support package of loans, scholarships, and grants than that available from a state school. If finances are a real consideration, you might be better off applying to the school with the lowest tuition, but it wouldn't hurt to apply to the small private school to see what kind of financial support it has to offer.

Other Factors

There are still some other factors to consider in shopping around for a medical school. For instance, does where you live play a big role in the school's selection process? Absolutely. State-supported medical schools are required by law to give preference to state residents, and as shown above, your tuition will be lower if you are a state resident than it will be if you live out of state. In addition there are many private schools that give preference to students who live in the state in which the school is located.

AAMC figures show that in recent years approximately two-thirds of all first-year students enrolled in schools in their own states: about 90 percent of the public school entrants and 43 percent of private school entrants. So if you are interested in enrolling in an out-of-state school, your chances for acceptance are definitely better in the smaller, private schools.

Second, if you are a woman or a member of a minority group, you need have no fear of encountering discriminatory policies in medical school. The situation for women is especially promising.

Between 1970 and 1994, the number of women physicians more than tripled until women comprised about 20 percent of all physicians in the United States. What's more, the total number of women first-year students has risen steadily from 38.5 percent in 1990–91 to 41.90 percent in 1994–95. At seventeen schools women make up 50 percent of all new entrants. In addition, the number of women faculty in U.S. medical schools has risen from 13.3 to 25 percent since 1968.

The situation with regard to minority students is likewise good. From 1990 to 1994 the number of accepted Black students increased from 1,146 to 1,427. Today there are a total of 2,014 minority first-year students in medical school and the Association of American Medical Colleges is redoubling its efforts to increase minority first-year entrants to 3,000 students by the year 2000. Besides efforts to cover recruitment and admissions, the AAMC is intensifying efforts to help students with serious financial and study difficulties to make the leap from college to medical school.

As to the number of medical schools to apply to, as noted above, students are currently applying to twelve medical schools apiece. You can well apply to more if you think it will help, but studies have shown that applying to more than twelve schools will not increase your chances of acceptance. Your best bet is to research the schools you want to apply to carefully and then narrow your list to a few well-considered schools.

Because there are so many aspects to consider in applying to medical school (not the least of which is meeting the various deadlines involved), at about the midyear point of your junior year you should ask your health professions adviser to help set up a schedule for submitting all of the various documents involved: MCAT results, grade point average and transcript of your college work, personal essay, letters of recommendation, and, of course, the applications to the various schools themselves.

AMCAS

Fortunately, the entire medical school admissions procedure has been speeded up in recent years through an agency known as AMCAS (American Medical

College Applications Service). In 1994, 101 of the 125 American medical schools participated, and 42,000 or 94 percent of all applicants applied to at least one AMCAS participating school. To apply to any of the participating schools, all you need to do is fill out one application and send it with one set of your official transcript to AMCAS. AMCAS will then duplicate the application and transcript and send them to the schools of your choice for a slight fee. The address of AMCAS is listed in Appendix B. For schools not participating in AMCAS, you must contact the admissions office directly for application procedures and materials.

Admissions Committees

What do admissions committees look at in evaluating your medical school credentials? For one, they are very interested in your motivation in selecting medicine as a career. Are you truly interested in serving others, or are you primarily interested in medicine for the wrong reasons? Do you believe it will enhance your image to drive a nice shiny Cadillac or Rolls-Royce as a result of the high earnings you expect to receive. Or are you interested in medicine because your father, mother, or grandparents were doctors—perhaps the worst reason of all for entering medicine.

To help evaluate your motivation and chances for success in medical school and in the career, the medical school will rely on two important sources of information: the personal statement, called for in nearly all applications, and a personal interview.

Personal statement.   Through the personal statement the committee wishes to learn about not only your reasons for wanting to study medicine, but your extracurricular activities and work achievements as well. Remember, the medical school is not necessarily looking for students who are tops in all of the premedical requirements—the natural sciences, math, and physics—and who have excellent grades, but little else to show for their efforts. They would much rather that you be a good student, one who is well rounded with interests in outside activities such as sports, music, journalism, and other extracurricular areas, or who is active in student government and other student concerns.

Personal Interview

In the personal interview the committee is seeking to find out if you are sincere and willing to make the commitment to the hours and effort that will be required to get your M.D. degree. Since the interview counts so heavily in your record, you should try to make sure to show yourself off to best advantage. Cleanliness and good grooming are important. Your shoes should be shined, and you should wear a suit, conservatively styled, preferably in blue or gray. This holds true for both men and women. The interview is not a time for showcasing your individuality by wearing loud or distracting clothing. Your clothes and appearance should not distract or detract; it is your answers to what the committee has to ask that count.

Serving as a hospital volunteer or caring for or visiting patients may be a tip-off of your willingness to serve the sick or impoverished.

Also important to the committee is your good judgment. Medicine can be very complex at times. For example, is it better to try to prolong the life of a cancer patient in her seventies and in a generally weakened and debilitated condition through some exhaustive and risky treatment, or would it be better to let her live out her life in whatever time is allotted? What can you tell parents who face financial stress and even ruin in trying to save the life of a child who is born with some debilitating defect such as muscular dystrophy?

This is the substance of medicine. How you answer these questions can make a real difference in the lives of your patients and their families. The committee will want to know how well you can withstand the stress of dealing with patients who are wracked with pain and so weakened and run down that it hurts to look at them. This, too, is a part of medicine.

Often patients will confide to a physician their deepest and most personal secrets regarding their finances, their jobs, their most sensitive problems with sex, their mates, or their children. How discreet are you? Can you be counted on to handle such information with the utmost tact and discretion?

These are a few of the questions you might be expected to field in the course of the interview. If uncertain of the answer to a question, it's better to be honest than to resort to guesswork or wrong answers. Nobody has all the answers, and you cannot be expected to know everything that is asked of you.

Often the medical school will try to accommodate you by grouping interviews at your convenience. Thus, for example, if you are asked to interview at several schools on the East Coast, usually the schools will work with you so that you can see all of them while you are in the area, rather than having to make a trip back at another time. This saves you a lot of time and money.

Rate of Acceptance

In 1995 only 38.2 percent of the candidates for medical school were accepted, a decrease over 1994 and a sign of the increased competition for spots. If accepted by two or more schools, you will be expected to accept the offer of the preferred school and notify the others of your decision. If in the future you should receive an offer from another school even more to your liking, you can then withdraw your first offer and take the offer of the preferred school.

Although admissions requirements for medical school are rough, the chances are excellent that once accepted you will complete the studies in good shape. According to the Council of Medical Education of the AMA, only 767 or 1.1 percent of all medical students withdrew in 1993–94. Some withdrew to transfer to another institution, for financial reasons, for poor academic performance, or for personal reasons. Another 2.4 percent of all students enrolled were on academic leave for poor academic performance so that they could work out problem areas of study or study for another degree.

MAKING THE MEDICAL CURRICULUM MORE RELEVANT

As noted in Chapter 1, the problems of the curriculum are elusive and in need of change to make the so-called basic science years more relevant to the practice of medicine. In recent years more and more schools have been experimenting with the basic science curriculum. Many are attempting to expose students to working with patients earlier in their studies. More and more schools are stressing the need of problem solving instead of the rote learning of factual information. They point out that it is more important to know how to solve a medical problem than to try to assimilate the vast body of medical knowledge, which grows larger almost every day.

Part of the problem can be traced to the fact that the traditional model of medical education stems from the Flexner Report, dating back to 1910. This model, which has been in place at most medical schools in the United States and Canada for the past seventy years, may have at one time served medicine very well, but it is showing its age and needs to be brought up to date to meet the changing needs of medical students.

The problem is an old one, as seen by the fact that in 1948 the AAMC appointed a panel of blue-ribbon medical educators to help update the curriculum to fit the needs of medicine in the twenty-first century. The panel found that "by concentrating on factual information, faculties have neglected to help students acquire the skills, values, and attitudes that are the foundation of a helping profession."

What Some Schools Are Doing

The schools are well aware of the problem and many have made innovations in teaching methods and in the way courses are presented, especially during the first two basic science years. At the University of Chicago's Pritzker School of Medicine, for instance, the clinical medicine program combines medical practice and basic science study. It was introduced more than twenty years ago, revised in 1987, and again in 1992.

The school also instituted a clinically based medical ethics program, which was integrated into the curriculum in 1967. It is one of only eleven schools in the United States that have been awarded grants by the Robert Wood Johnson Foundation to plan for educational reform by revamping the curriculum and reviewing some of the basic beliefs on which the curriculum is based.

Rush Medical College, also based in Chicago, revamped its curriculum in 1984 by offering students an alternative to the traditional curriculum. The two-year alternative program stresses problem solving in small group learning and in independent study. Students working in small independent groups seek out faculty members on their own initiative. Instead of reading assignments, the students do library research to get pertinent facts and then contact faculty members who act as resources in backing up and supporting their findings.

Harvard's New Pathway program introduces medical students to the clinics and hospitals early in their training in small increments during their basic science years. Other schools have followed along the same lines and some may introduce still more radical changes along these lines.

Not all of the experimentation deals with improving teaching methods or making the curriculum more meaningful. During the early 1990s, the UCLA medical school introduced a program aimed at making students more "compassionate." It features visits to drug rehabilitation centers and juvenile jails and it involves student interaction with actors playing the part of patients.

Specific Changes

But change has been relatively modest and slow. Schools vary considerably on how they teach the courses in the first two years, but almost always the program is based on the basic sciences: anatomy, biochemistry, physiology, microbiology, pharmacology, pathology, and behavioral sciences. The courses may be taught independently by department or on a team basis featuring faculty from various basic science and clinical departments. In almost all schools, introducing clinical problems or working with actual patients comes early on. During their first year students start to learn how to interview and examine patients. In other schools the first clinical contact may consist of faculty discussions featuring real patients.

The last two years, the so-called clinical years, are spent studying patients in various clinical settings, usually in the hospital. Here the student attempts to establish good doctor-patient contacts and learns how to conduct a medical examination, take a patient history, and recognize the more familiar disease symptoms.

Here, too, the student begins rotations through a series of what are termed clinical clerkships in several areas of medicine, usually including obstetrics-gynecology, internal medicine, pediatrics, psychiatry, and surgery. Clerkships can vary in length from two to twelve weeks.

Usually students are given the job of working up or gathering data on a given number of patients per week and presenting their findings to the faculty. They work with the residents (post-M.D. trainees) as well as doctors in discharging their duties.

Then, in the last year, students often are allowed to take electives in the various specialties and subspecialties and in alternative methods of training—in community clinics or the emergency room, for instance. Some students work directly under the tutelage of a senior staff physician while others do laboratory work.

Often, as a result of the contacts they have made during their clinical years and their exposure to various specialists and their specialties, students make their decisions on what areas of medicine they want to specialize in.

Examinations

In all schools some form of comprehensive exam is required to see how well students have integrated medical knowledge and practice. Currently eighty-seven schools report that they require students to pass Step 1 of the United

States Medical Licensing Examination (USMLE) at the end of their basic science years in order to graduate. And fifty-nine schools report that they currently require students to pass Step 2 of the USMLE to graduate.

The USMLE is a three-step examination required for licensure and often for medical school graduation. Step 1 evaluates students' understanding of basic biomedical principles; Step 2 assesses medical knowledge and ability to integrate such knowledge in clinical practice; Step 3, given after graduation, evaluates the ability of the graduate to apply what he or she has learned in medical school. (See Chapter 5 for a more detailed discussion of the USMLE.)

Alternatives to the Traditional Curriculum

It should be emphasized that several alternatives to the traditional medical program are offered in many medical schools. There are first of all the combined bachelor and medical programs where a limited number of students, based on their high school performance, are permitted to complete all of the requirements for the combined program in six or seven years.

Research. Most schools are receptive to allowing students to work on research projects. Programs ranging from several months to a year often can be arranged to help students explore their creative talents for biomedical research.

Medical Scientist Training Program (MSTP). In recognition of the need for medical scientists trained in both the clinical and basic sciences, the National Institute of General Medical Sciences sponsors the MSTP program at thirty-three schools. About 175 spots are currently being supported. Each provides a maximum of six years of support and includes a stipend of $10,008 a year. For information about this highly competitive program contact:

> Program Administrator
> Medical Scientist Training Program
> National Institutes of Health
> 45 Center Drive, MSC 6200
> Bethesda, MD 20892-6200
> Phone: (301) 594-5560

In addition to these special programs, a few schools offer M.D.-Ph.D. and M.D.-J.D. degrees. For information on these programs check the *Medical School Admission Requirements* directory, issued annually by the Association of American Medical Colleges for a nominal fee.

CANADIAN MEDICAL EDUCATION

For the most part, admission policies of Canadian medical schools are very similar to those of U.S. schools. But since the requirements for admission do vary slightly, it is advisable to check the *Medical School Admission Requirements* directory.

Fourteen of the Canadian medical schools now have four-year programs, like that of most U.S. schools. McMaster and Calgary, however, have three-year programs.

All Canadian schools, with the exception of McGill University in Montreal, take a few students from the United States. The MCAT is required for admission in eleven of the sixteen Canadian schools.

Age, sex, race, or religion are not factors in gaining admission, although fewer older candidates are admitted than younger ones. As is true of the United States, the number of women applicants to Canadian medical schools has seen dramatic growth in recent years. For further information about admission requirements, programs, and Canadian medical schools, contact the Association of Canadian Medical Colleges (see Appendix B).

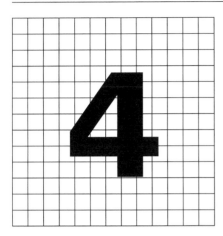

FINANCING A
MEDICAL EDUCATION

Okay, you've applied to several medical schools, been accepted by one or two, and, perhaps, if you're very smart, you've been accepted by three schools. You're all set—right? Not quite, for as we have seen in Chapter 3, the medical curriculum is a bumpy one, and you will be sorely pressed to keep up with your studies and to meet the powerful academic requirements.

In addition to your studies, you have one additional obstacle to overcome, and it is a big one—paying for or financing your medical education. If you are independently wealthy or have wealthy parents, this might not be a problem. However, not many medical students are in this category. Most must search around to see how the medical education bill—which, as we have seen, is considerable—is going to be paid.

As noted previously, medical school tuition and fees averaged $22,874 in 1994–1995 in private schools and $8,760 in public schools (much more if you live out of state). These are very impressive figures, and you will be hard put to make ends meet during your medical school years. But it can be done and is being done almost daily, so there is no reason to believe that it will be otherwise for you. If you have the brainpower and the academic record to support your education, funds will be available to pay for medical school; you can count on it.

But it may mean making do with a lot less on your part—like living in a dormitory instead of an apartment, for instance. Your school will help, but they want to make sure that you have exhausted your own personal funds before they dip into their own limited resources.

In almost all instances, you will have to establish need if you want to qualify for any of several federally sponsored loan programs. To establish need, your family's contributions and resources will be subtracted from the school's standard student budget. How much your family is expected to contribute is determined through use of a national needs analysis service such as the Graduate and Professional Financial Aid Service (GAPFAS), the College Scholarship Service (CSS), or the American College Testing program (ACT). Support material, such as the most recent family and student tax returns, are usually required even for older or married students.

For students who had to finance the cost of their medical education, loans provided the bulk of the assistance (79 percent) in 1994. The balance (21 percent) came from scholarships, grants, and work-study programs.

Of those who had to rely on outside sources of financial assistance, the average debt of all students reported was $63,000.

Right here and now, you should shed any inhibitions you may have had in the past or may still have about borrowing money. More than 79 percent of all students enrolled in medical school currently carry some debt. So, you can see that you will be in good company if you have to borrow to pay for at least part of your medical education.

TRIMMING EXPENSES

Before even attempting to get financial assistance, you must make sure that you have pared down expenses to the bone. For instance, have you considered living at home (if you are attending a local medical school)? Here is one good way to trim expenses. But you also must consider if living at home will create conflicts, requests for household assistance, and so forth, that you would not get were you to live elsewhere. How far will you have to commute from home to school and back? Long-distance travel in traffic can take a lot of time—time that is very valuable.

Here are several other questions to ask yourself. Is dormitory living cheaper? Are there dorms for graduates and are they reasonably quiet? Do most medical students live off campus, and if so, is this through preference? Is off-campus housing in safe areas? If you live in a cold climate, are heating and electrical costs included in your rent? These are just a few of the questions that you should ask yourself. Besides housing you should also take into account transportation, food, and personal expenses.

Consider for example that under transportation, the government will not allow you to purchase a car with federal loans. Also, a low-cost car is a possibility only if the school's financial officer decides that off-campus living requires that you travel long distances to get to clinical teaching facilities. Here are a few other ways that you can trim your expenses:

- Share apartments and rides.
- Buy through food co-ops.
- Buy used books, instruments, and lab coats.

- Work while in medical school. This may not be possible, but some jobs, such as a graduate assistantship, can often be handled during off hours and will help pay your bills.
- Look for opportunities to house sit, baby sit, or pet sit.
- If you have talents in such areas as flower arranging, singing, or playing an instrument, for example, try to parlay them into part-time jobs for extra income.

GETTING FINANCIAL HELP

Ranking right up with trimming costs is the financial package available from the school. While exploring the financial support offered by various schools to which you are applying, here are a few questions you should be asking:

- What is the average debt of students who are completing their studies at the school?
- How many students at the school are presently working?
- Does the school have an emergency loan program? If so, how much can you borrow and how quickly can you get funds?
- Does the school have a loan forgiveness program to help students with massive debts?
- How many students have had to leave school for financial reasons?

If you find yourself in the fortunate position of having been accepted by several schools, a visit to your two top choices and the answers you get to the following questions will help you make your decision.

- What resources does the school have (low-interest loans and scholarship)? This is especially important when deciding between a public and a private school.
- In the financial package offered, are any of the funds packaged with high-interest federal loans?
- If the financial package is good for the first year, can the school be counted on to offer an equally attractive package in the years that follow?
- Does the school offer merit scholarships to students? If so what are the qualifications and for how many years are they in effect?

Usually the financial aid package offered by your school is a mix of loans and scholarships. The loans are offered primarily through several federal loan sources. Some scholarships may be offered by the school and others are available from various community or private organizations that support students of a certain ethnic background or whose parents work for certain employers.

Federal Loan Programs   Specifically here are several funds available primarily though federal loan programs:

Obtained through the school:

- Stafford Student Loan (state guaranteed-loan program—subsidized and unsubsidized)
- Perkins Loan (national defense student loan)
- Supplemental Loan for Students (SLS)
- Health Education Assistance Loan (HEAL)

All of the above loans are based on need except for the Stafford unsubsidized, SLS, and HEAL funds, which are based on cost.

All of these programs vary considerably on such characteristics as borrowing limits, interest rates, when interest is accrued, when repayment kicks in, grace period, deferments, and so forth. So it is very important that you consider these carefully in deciding which you will accept, assuming that you have a choice.

The Stafford Student Loan for example, which offers a maximum of $8,500 a year, provides the foundation for nearly all student loan programs.

So it is definitely to your interest to know which loan funds are being offered. Some schools offer only HEAL because they have no other funds available. Others have Perkins as well as Stafford Loans available, which are available to everyone and which carry a much lower rate of interest.

Several other facts are worth noting at this point regarding loans, since they impact greatly on medical school bills. For one, paying for a medical education has become easier and cheaper for the more than 52,000 medical students who rely on loans to help pay for their schooling. Now the Student Loan Marketing Association (known as Sallie Mae) will help to reduce the cost of student loans as the newest member of the MEDLOANS program, a comprehensive student loan program sponsored by the Association of American Medical Colleges (AAMC) to answer specific financing needs of medical students. Under this program students who take out MEDLOANS now can participate in Sallie Mae's borrower benefit features including Direct Repay, Great Rewards, and Great Returns. For example, a medical student with $64,000 in loans—the current national average for medical students—can save more than 7 percent through these incentive programs. How? Through a combination of interest rate reductions and credits to the loan principal. Also, MEDLOANS participants will be able to take advantage of graduated and income-sensitive payment schedules to make repayment of their debt easier. Sallie Mae has long been the nation's leading provider of loans for college students' needs. Combined with Sallie Mae's participation with MEDLOANS is a long-term commitment by all program participants that further enhances the program's utility. Now in its tenth year, MEDLOANS has provided more than $1.3 billion of uninterrupted and affordable loan funds for medical students. For information on the program, contact the Association of American Medical Colleges at the address listed in Appendix B.

Besides these funds, each of the armed forces—the army, navy, and air force—offers a limited number of service scholarship programs. A typical program is that of the air force, which pays full tuition, a monthly living stipend, and a book allowance. But at the same time, you are obligated under terms of the programs for a year's service for each year of support. For information on each of these extremely competitive programs, refer to the respective organizations:

Air Force: Medical Recruiting Division, HQ USAFR/RSHM
550 D Street West, Suite 1
Randolph AFB, TX 78150-4527

Army: U.S. Army Health Professions Support Agency SPS-PD
5109 Leesburg Pike
Falls Church, VA 22041-3258

Navy: Commander, Navy Recruiting Command
801 North Randolph
Arlington, VA 22203-1991

Another program worth noting is the National Health Service Corps, open to qualified medical students who wish to practice in medically underserved areas in inner city or rural areas.

The program offers both scholarships and loans. Scholarships cover tuition, books, and fees as well as a monthly stipend. In return you agree to serve one year for each year of the award in a medically underserved area.

Also available are loans of up to $25,000 for the first two years and up to $35,000 for every year thereafter. For information on the program contact:

National Health Service Corps Scholarship Program
U.S. Public Health Recruitment
8201 Greensboro Drive
Suite 600
McLean, VA 22102

Scholarships

Scholarships, a primary source of funding for more than half of all medical students, are available through several sources: the medical schools, which may have several scholarships available through charitably minded individuals; corporations; foundations; and several federal programs. Other scholarships are restricted to students of a given ethnic, religious, or racial group, or from a given community or state. There are literally hundreds of such scholarships. It may involve some legwork and research to find these, but the effort will be worthwhile since you may well qualify for one or more of them.

The chances are also good that the medical school has a number of private loan funds available to qualified students, which can also be useful.

Repaying a Loan

Here's something to consider: A good reason to keep a tight rein on debt obligation is fear of the unknown. Although there is some certainty of obtaining a residency position that will allow you to pay off at least part of your debt, it is quite likely that your salary during residency, which is when most loan repayment goes into effect, will not keep pace with inflation.

In 1994–95 salaries for medical residents averaged $30,686 for those in their first year of residency to $38,472 for those in their sixth year, according to the Association of American Medical Colleges.

Here's a typical example of what could happen if you're not careful. Following the completion of a three-year residency, a new doctor accepts a position that will pay her $68,000 for the first year. For the third year of her residency, she will be required to pay a monthly loan repayment of $412. This may not seem much based on her monthly salary of $5,666 but in reality it will take a big bite out of her income when added to other living expenses and consumer debts. Repayment is a factor that must be figured in any loan application that you consider.

In summary, then, bear in mind that either through your school's resources or your own efforts, financing is available. But it will not automatically fall into your lap, no matter how good a student you are. It will take a little research and effort, but if you persevere, you will find the financial support that you need.

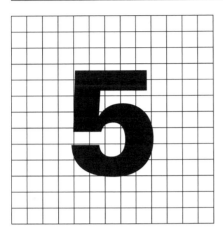

CHOOSING A SPECIALTY AND LANDING A MEDICAL RESIDENCY

Now that you're in medical school, you might think that you could concentrate on your studies and let it go at that, right? Wrong. At this point you are called upon to make quite possibly the most important decision of all, a decision that could well determine how happy you will be in your medical career: your choice of specialty.

A recent AMA survey showed that 25 percent of practicing physicians, given what they know about medicine, would most likely not have gone to medical school; 14 percent said they definitely would have elected another career. Added to the 1 percent who said they were unsure, this comes to staggering 40 percent of practicing physicians who believed that they might be better off in another profession.

But before slamming the door shut on a medical career, you might also consider that few if any careers offer the options that medicine does. For instance, if you like to find quick solutions to the problems that confront your patient, you might consider surgery or ophthalmology. Or, if you prefer to build lasting relationships with your patients, you could opt for primary care, perhaps internal medicine, pediatrics, or psychiatry. Perhaps you would like more control over your hours and are technically minded, then radiology or pathology are specialties that you might want to look into.

Medicine offers a wide and often confusing array of choices for people of varying skills and needs, and it's not getting any simpler. Currently there are twenty-four board-approved specialties and approximately sixty-six subspecialties, and the list keeps growing larger every year. It's easy to see how making the wrong specialty choice might sour you on the profession and make you want to drop out of medicine.

Training in each of these twenty-four specialty areas and in the sixty-six other subspecialties is conducted in more than a thousand institutions throughout the nation, primarily large, acute-care hospitals. These programs will be discussed in Chapter 10. For now, let's focus on the problem of selecting a medical specialty.

SELECTING A MEDICAL SPECIALTY

In seeking a specialty, consider the various factors that reflect your own interests and skills. Medical students considering a choice of specialties have indicated the following factors as most important in forming their own choice: 81 percent believed that time available for their family and personal lives was important; 53 percent listed as a major consideration the need for professional independence; 29 percent considered the personal income offered; 29 percent listed the possibility of incurring medical malpractice suits as an important factor; and 10 percent indicated that the chances of contracting AIDS was yet another serious consideration. Other factors that have influenced many students in deciding upon medical careers were "opportunities to use special talents and abilities."

Although the opportunity to make an adequate income is an important and certainly a legitimate consideration, your decision should not be based solely, or even primarily, on the prospect of earning a lot of money. For one thing, medicine is changing radically. Surgery, which used to be the area of medicine offering the biggest bucks, is reaching the saturation point, especially in such highly specialized areas as neurosurgery and cardiovascular surgery. True, there will always be opportunities for those who are specially talented in these areas, but the competition in these and in other areas of surgery can be expected to increase in the near future.

On the other hand, primary care, including internal medicine and family practice, which used to rate the lowest on the salary totem pole, is coming up strong. Because of this demand for qualified professionals, an increase in salary potential is expected in years to come.

So earnings potential, though important, should not bear undue weight in your specialty considerations. More important is your personality. You may not, for instance, have the emotional makeup or the aptitude to make the grade in surgery. And rather than risk a lifetime of dissatisfaction and unhappiness in your choice of work, you might be much better off choosing a specialty that pays a little less but is more emotionally attuned to your needs.

Consider that between 60 and 75 percent of all medical students change specialties during medical school, while 20 percent of all residents switch to other medical specialties. Another 16 percent of practicing physicians change specialties at some time or other during their careers.

Rather than risk finding yourself unhappy and dissatisfied midway through your career, you should make a special effort in the choice of a specialty that will guard against this possibility and pay off in increased personal satisfaction and career growth.

**Evaluating Your
Strengths, Aptitudes,
and Interests**

How do you go about choosing a specialty that matches your needs and personality most accurately? This is a tough decision. To start with, you need to ask yourself some questions to evaluate your strengths and aptitudes as well as your interests. Do you, for instance, enjoy working with patients for the long haul, building long-term relationships with them over the years; or would you prefer to see medical problems resolved quickly? In the first case, you would probably do well in primary care, and in the second, you might be better off selecting surgery. Next, you should look over the various specialties listed in Chapter 10 to see which ones seem to match your personality and needs the most. This being done, you need to gather as much information as you can about the specialties that appeal to you, and then through reading and actual experience, confirm your first impressions or reject them based on fact rather than initial reactions or emotions.

Let's face it, most medical students choose a specialty as part of the round of clinical clerkships that they encounter in the third year of medical school. About halfway through the third year, for better or worse, most students have made a choice and are involved in the complex and often frustrating problem of finding a residency that will give them the training they need for licensure and certification as a specialist.

Although this procedure has worked to both the student's and the profession's advantage, it nevertheless can be and often is misleading, since it is based on limited exposure and choice of settings. Usually students choose a specialty because of what they see in this very limited setting, or because they form a favorable impression of a given physician, resident, team or selection of patients. Or based on this very limited exposure, it may be just the reverse, and students will form a very negative or distorted picture of a specialty due to some uncharacteristic or exaggerated experience, which can spoil their appreciation of a given specialty.

Also, traditionally, clinical rotations offered in most schools are limited to such fields as internal medicine, surgery, pediatrics, neurology, obstetrics, and psychiatry. In the past these were the specialties of greatest demand and popularity. However, in recent years some of these fields have become highly competitive and hence may not offer the career potential they once did, according to a recent survey of the AMA.

Gastroenterology, cardiology, and anesthesiology, according to a recent report of the American Medical Association, are among the specialties showing surpluses in the number of practitioners. However, several specialties that seem to offer the highest potential according to the report, such as physical medicine and rehabilitation, preventive medicine, and emergency medicine, are seldom included in the clinical rotations offered to third-year medical students.

So how do you get a good handle on your interests, likes, and aptitudes for medicine? Probably a method that is as easy to follow as any is to be found in the book: *How to Choose a Medical Specialty* by Anita Taylor. This book, which you may have in your medical school library, provides short profiles of each of the major specialties and subspecialties broken down according to the various considerations in making a decision and followed by a self-assessment quiz for each. After ranking the various self-assessment quizzes, you can see where you scored the highest and make your choice accordingly.

A somewhat similar self-evaluation quiz is offered by Kenneth Iserson in his excellent book *Getting into a Residency*. Iserson offers a Personal Trait Analysis, which lists forty traits or characteristics that he asks readers to fill out according to those they like, those in which they have strengths and may also like, or those in which they have no particular strengths or weaknesses. He then breaks these traits down into a list that rates them as High Priority, as Priority, as Acceptable, and as Reject.

This somewhat complex system, while useful in matching the major specialties to your own talents and interests, does not rank the subspecialties of each, which in some cases differ quite a bit in the skills and aptitudes called for. For example, the work of a cardiologist, who may do cardiac catheterization and other heart diagnostic tests, will differ considerably in the skills required and the type of work performed than the average internist, who will not ordinarily do this kind of procedure.

Other resources that may prove helpful in choosing a specialty are the Glaxo Pathway Evaluation course offered at some medical schools that offers a self-evaluation handout and the Meyers-Briggs Indicator or the Medical Specialty Preference Indicator. The latter in particular shows how your interests stack up with those of physicians in the various medical specialties.

In addition, specialty information is available from some journals published by the AMA and from the Council on Medical Specialties (see address listed in Appendix B), and *New Physician* runs a yearly review of the medical specialties, which is very useful. Then, too, the specialty societies themselves (see Appendix B) can be very helpful in supplying information on the specialty in question.

Finally, rundowns on recognized specialties and subspecialties can be found in the brochure, *Which Medical Specialty for You?*, published by the American Board of Medical Specialties (see Appendix B for their address). The ABMS also publishes a brochure, *Medical Specialty Certification and Related Matters*, which gives information about medicine as a profession and about specialty certification for the medical student, the resident, and others, as well as a list of sources of additional information.

Evaluating Potential Earnings

As noted earlier one of the primary considerations in choosing a specialty is the opportunity to earn a good income. This is especially important in the light of the rising cost of medical practice, particularly the cost of malpractice insurance, and the very considerable debt with which the average student leaves medical school. As noted in Chapter 4, this debt approached $63,000 in 1994, a 50 percent increase over 1989 and an increase of better than 115 percent over 1981 costs.

Small wonder why the chance of earning a good salary becomes an important consideration in rating the various specialties. As has been true in the past and is still true today, the surgical specialties pay more because their reimbursement schedules are based on the concept, rightly or wrongly, that procedural activities (certain *doing* procedures) rate higher payment than those involving *cognitive* procedures (those involving analysis of data to determine diagnosis and treatment). Ordinarily cognitive skills are associated with primary care specialists such as the internist, pediatrician, and family or general practitioner.

Such was the case, but in recent years several other factors have come into play that may change this method of payment considerably. For one there is the Resource Based Relative Value Scale (RBRVS), which Medicare and other third-party payers use as a guide in their reimbursement of physicians. Under this system, a combination of factors such as time spent with patients, cost of the physician's training, and cost of practice are all considered. Although the AMA estimates that most (about 75 percent) of current physicians would either gain or not be affected, there would be winners and losers under this system. Rates paid to surgeons, pathologists, and radiologists, for instance, would be expected to drop considerably, while those for family physicians, internists, and psychiatrists would go up appreciably. But to a great extent, the present gap between income of surgeons on the one hand and generalists, or internists on the other, would still exist.

Also expected to impact seriously on physician income is the relatively recent introduction of what are termed Diagnostic Related Groups (DRGs), in which the federal government, in such programs as Medicare and Medicaid, has established rates for most diagnoses and diseases based on norms of practice.

These then become the basis of rates paid to the physician and to other health care providers including hospitals. If the physician's charges are lower than or in line with these standard rates, he or she will break even or even make money on various patients. If, however, there are unanticipated problems or the costs are higher than anticipated, the doctor must pay for these higher charges out of his or her pocket and is limited to only the amount called for by the DRG.

In short, while surgeons have traditionally been the top revenue earners in medicine and still are to a great extent, forces are afoot that may well change the entire pay picture in a few years, and this could help to close the current revenue gap between the various medical specialties.

Evaluating Future Demand

One other factor that should be taken into account is the anticipated demand for various medical specialists in the future. Here it must be confessed the picture is somewhat confusing to put it mildly.

There are those, for instance, who believe that within the next fifteen to twenty years there will be a serious personnel shortage that will affect all branches of medicine. Those who hold this belief theorize that the demand for various practitioners will increase as the supply decreases. They point to various trends that have fueled the demand for physicians: more people living to a ripe old age, with a corresponding increase in the demand for medical services as citizens become more vulnerable to disease and sickness; elimination of many former killers, such as polio and diphtheria, with a corresponding elimination of factors that tend to shorten the life span; and increased demand for services as more and more citizens come under insurance coverage through programs offered by various third-party payers, HMOs, alternative health care plans, and, of course, the federal government.

All of these factors indicate an increasing demand for doctors in all specialties. Certainly a strong influence will be the impact of medical technology. For instance, the availability of such diagnostic tests as cardiac catheterization has fired the demand for cardiologists with the skills to perform these services; availability of bypass surgery has touched off a widespread demand for cardiovascular surgeons trained in this procedure; and the availability of other diagnostic tests such as CT-scans, MRIs, and nuclear scans has fueled the demand for radiologists able to perform these tests.

Despite this uncertainty, it seems safe to say that within the next ten to twenty years there will be a vastly expanded need for physicians with credentials in primary care—pediatrics, internal medicine, geriatrics, preventive medicine, and adolescent psychiatry—while demand will taper down and even create surpluses in such fields as cardiology, gastroenterology, and anesthesia. Even so, those who excel in even the latter specialties can expect to find employment.

Test Driving a Specialty   Taking all these factors into consideration—earnings, all the factors that can influence payment schedules, and anticipated demand for physicians—what's the next step in choosing a specialty? It involves gathering information and experiencing your specialty of interest. And here, right at the outset, one of the most important things you can do is to choose a mentor or adviser. This person can make a big difference in guiding your career by cluing you into options that you might otherwise miss and helping you to surmount the confusing and gray areas of medicine.

Ask around, especially of those who themselves are going through the clinical circuit, as to who the top-notch teachers are. Try to select as your adviser one who is primarily a teacher, rather than someone involved largely in research, which can affect his or her accessibility as an adviser.

The truly top-notch mentors are teachers who are concerned with the futures of their students—who want them to succeed at all costs. Such a person will make a great adviser.

Try to select someone from a field similar to the one you are thinking of entering. A pediatrician or one specializing in geriatrics is not too far removed from an internist, but a radiologist or a pathologist is worlds removed from an internist, in most respects.

Now look for opportunities to test your career choices. One of the best ways is to volunteer for clinical service during your free time—during lunch, for instance, or on a Saturday or Sunday morning. Your adviser can help if he or she is in the clinical field in which you are interested; if not, he or she may be able to put you in touch with the person who has the authority to let you volunteer.

Here is an excellent way to see how things are going. Do the people in the field—the specialists—seem happy in what they are doing? Does the field seem to offer the opportunity for professional growth, fulfillment, and income that you seek? What drawbacks, if any, can you detect? The sooner you get involved in a field of interest, the better your chances to really learn what the field is all about.

Here is also a fine opportunity to test out your basic science studies by seeing how they apply in a clinical setting. In short, here is a chance to check the relevance of basic sciences in a real-life clinical setting.

Talk to as many physicians in your specialty of interest as you can. Try to observe them in their office, with patients, or in a clinical setting, hospital, or nursing home, for instance, so you can see how they operate in different settings. There is no better way to find out what the field entails than talking to the physicians involved and observing them at work under various conditions.

GETTING THE RESIDENCY MOST SUITED TO YOU

Once you have decided on which specialty you would like to practice in, you are ready to concentrate on the task of getting a residency, which is very important because you cannot be certified or licensed without having a residency under your belt.

There are a few things you should do while still in medical school to make sure you get the residency most suited to your needs and abilities. And here the question of grades—specifically honors grades, usually the equivalent of an A average, or 4.0 on a scale of 1 to 4—comes into play. Although grades are important in all aspects of medical school, they are especially important in certain areas if you expect to get the residency most suited to your interests. Therefore, you must make a special effort to pass with honors in these areas.

If your school is one of the many that are on the Pass/Fail system, you will have to rely on other ways of displaying your academic ability—such as special awards and letters of recommendation, for example.

The courses or areas of concentration that are crucial are listed in order of importance, as follows:

1. Third-Year Clinical Clerkships. Unlike your experience in the basic science years, where courses and approaches can vary considerably, the experience attained during the clinical years is very similar in most medical schools. Thus your work can be quite readily compared by residency directors reviewing your credentials.

2. Senior Specialty Clerkships. This clerkship is next in importance to your performance during the junior clerkships. It is especially important to take a clerkship in a specialty of your choice in a major teaching hospital that is known and respected by residency directors.

3. Basic Science or Preclinical Years. These are especially important if you are leaning toward pathology, since pathology is required in just about all schools in the preclinical years.

One final note about honors. You don't necessarily have to be a genius to rate honors in any given course, but it does take effort and plenty of it. Extra effort in the form of coming in early for clinical rounds and staying late can prove your dedication and earn commendations from the house staff.

Other efforts that can pay off include extracurricular reading in the area of your clerkship or assignment and studying diligently for any exams that may be required at the end of your clerkship. It is that student who shows his or her willingness to go the extra mile whose efforts will pay off, all other things being equal.

Another way to ensure that you get the residency of your choice is to do well on the United States Medical Licensing Exam, the three-step examination for medical licensure in the United States that replaces the Federation Licensing Examination (FLEX). Each step measures your comprehension of the medical education curriculum. Step 1, for instance, given at the end of the basic science years, assesses if you understand and can apply key concepts in biomedical sciences while step 2, given at the end of the clinical years, measures your medical knowledge and your understanding of clinical science in providing for patient care. Step 3, given after graduation from medical school, measures not only your comprehension of medical science, but your ability to apply that knowledge in a clinical setting.

Although these exams are used officially for licensure to practice medicine in just about all states, they are also used by many, if not most, of the residency programs in evaluating your credentials. An estimated 60 percent of all residency programs want to see how well you have performed in step 1 of the United States Medical Licensing Examination, usually taken at the end of your sophomore year. And an estimated 40 percent of all residency programs consider how well you perform in step 2, taken in either April or September of your junior year. Note that currently the exam can be taken only by graduates of officially accredited medical schools in the United States or Canada; this excludes foreign medical students or graduates.

The importance of each of these exams cannot be overemphasized as many residency program directors rely heavily on how well you do on the tests to screen applicants. It is probably the most objective evidence of your ability and attainment in medicine, is much more reliable than dean's letters or other reference letters, and is doubly important if your school is on the Pass/Fail system. Unless you can reach a minimum level considered acceptable by the residency program involved (which varies from one specialty to another), you most likely will not be accepted for the program.

The USMLE has superseded the National Board of Medical Examiners (NBME) as a barometer of how well you have done in medical school, and it is anticipated to be as effective in screening applicants as was the NBME.

Besides clinical work and striving hard to earn honors in courses that can make the difference in your efforts to get a residency, consider using your summer vacation to familiarize yourself with the world of clinical medicine. Such a move would make an excellent escape from the regimentation of class-work and would give you a good opportunity to practice medicine, even in a very restricted scale. Ask your adviser or the student affairs office to help you locate summer vacation opportunities in clinical settings.

Note that research, though not essential in obtaining most residencies, can help in some areas where the competition is especially rough, such as emergency medicine, ophthalmology, or orthopedics. But if research is not your forte, don't worry about it for now. Other opportunities will arise later, after you have landed a residency. You can reevaluate your thinking about research at that time.

A few more words about preparing for the residency while in medical school are in order before we go on to the next step. One important question that is constantly being debated concerns the need for taking a senior clerkship in your specialty choice. Those opposed to this way of thinking say that it makes no sense to duplicate the training you will receive during the residency itself. But if you are a topflight student, such a clerkship could help to prove that you have what it takes to succeed in this area—not just the paper attributes. If, on the other hand, your grades are not quite up to par, you will need to do more than just pass—you will need top grades in your senior clerkship year to rate consideration for a residency.

Gathering Information about Residencies

At this point you are ready to obtain all of the information available about the residencies available in your specialty of interest. Such information includes what the residencies are like, how tough they are to get into, and the options available for completing the program.

The two major sources of information on all specialty residency programs should be available through the student affairs office at your medical school. First of all an annually updated computer program, the AMA *Fellowship and Residency Electronic Interactive Database Access* system, otherwise known as FREIDA, provides information on such items as characteristics of faculty and residents, call schedules, benefits provided, curriculum, shared-schedule positions available, and much more.

The *Directory of Graduate Education Programs*, usually referred to as the Green Book, is also annually updated by the AMA. Though not as detailed as the information listed in FREIDA, this book provides information not on the computer at present, including requirements for program accreditation, statistics on graduate medical information, specialty certification requirements, and so forth.

Also helpful in providing additional information not included in either of the above directories is the *Medical Education* issue of the *Journal of the American Medical Association*, usually available in late summer or early fall. It offers a complete rundown of residency programs available, total positions and first-year positions available in the specialty, subspecialty and combined specialty residency programs, programs and residents on duty, and much more. All programs shown are accredited by the Accreditation Council for Graduate Medical Education (ACGME). There were 7,347 accredited programs at the end of 1994.

In the fall of your senior year you will receive the *NRMP* (*National Residency Matching Program*) directory via the dean's office, which lists the programs participating in the Match, described later in this chapter. This book describes how the Match works, code numbers and number of positions being offered, and worksheets and forms needed to participate in the Book. The *NRMP Results* book gives the previous year's results and should be available in your school library and/or the student affairs office.

The Council of Teaching Hospitals Directory, published annually by the AAMC and available through that organization, offers much more detailed information about the residencies offered by members of the council than that found in the Green Book.

The *American Hospital Association Guide to the Health Care Field*, published by the AHA, offers information on the seven-thousand member hospitals of the association. Though most are not primary or base teaching hospitals, a good part of your training could be received in many of these hospitals, and hence this could be a very helpful reference.

The Council of Teaching Hospitals conducts an annual survey of stipends, benefits, and funding for house staff, which can be helpful in evaluating residency programs. It is available from the AAMC.

Then, too, five specialties—family practice, psychiatry, preventive medicine, critical care medicine, and physical medicine and rehabilitation—publish detailed information about residency programs offered in each specialty. And the American Medical Student Association publishes *Student Guide to the Appraisal and Selection of House Staff Training Programs,* which is loaded with information on resumes, letters of recommendation, interviewing, and so forth.

For information about residencies in each specialty, write to the individual specialty society involved at the address shown in Appendix B.

What to Look for in a Residency

The primary factor in considering residencies offered at a facility is the clinical experience offered—both in number and type of patients and setting. Find out the ratio of residents to patients seen. There can be too many residents to get any meaningful experience or too few residents, which means that you will not have adequate time to evaluate patients and to discuss possible diagnoses and treatments. Similarly, setting is important. In a large teaching hospital there may be too few attending physicians and too many patients; in the community hospital, just the opposite may be true.

On-call schedules.   Although recent court rulings have tended to liberalize on-call schedules, there are still many programs where night call every other night is still common. Get the facts so that you can properly evaluate this very important issue.

Geographical location.   If you are married, this can be a major consideration if your spouse's work is limited to any given area. If you're single, the only geographical restrictions are your own personal preferences.

Faculty.   Are the faculty vitally interested in teaching? Are there enough of them to do the job? Also, are there adequate opportunities in research to help you measure your interest in this area and stay abreast of what is happening in the field?

Other considerations.   Another key issue involves opportunities to be exposed to a given area of a specialty that may be of interest, such as obstetrical anesthesiology as part of an anesthesiology residency. You will also want to explore local job prospects open after training; rules and benefits of health coverage for you and your family, if this applies; and insurance coverage. Other benefits you will want to look into involve life and disability insurance, free parking, childcare (if you have children), and opportunities to moonlight. Salaries for house staff vary by section of the country and from private to public hospitals, which generally pay less. So be sure to check this as well.

How and Where to Apply   The number of programs to which to apply will depend on the specialty. Generally the more competitive the program, the more programs you should apply to. According to the AAMC, 48 percent of all medical students applied to six to fifteen programs and 21.5 percent applied to sixteen to twenty-five programs. By contacting a number of programs, you can choose the ones that best match your needs; or if you go through the Match program, you can select the programs of greatest appeal and hope that you get your preference.

In requesting information about the programs that interest you, you will invariably receive a package containing information about the program and materials required, which can vary considerably from one program to another. You will also receive the required application. While a few programs use what is known as a Uniform Application Form, most prefer that you fill out the application and send it with the materials requested—dean's letter, other reference letters, medical school and undergraduate transcripts, and other information.

Generally, the earlier you get the information sent in, the better. Many programs have only so many slots for interviews, and if you wait too long (beyond August or September of your senior year), you may miss out on an interview.

Ask for a letter or recommendation from at least one faculty member of your chosen specialty. Other letters should come from faculty members who know you and can write enthusiastically about your abilities. If a teacher seems hesitant about writing a letter, forget about it and ask someone else. If a faculty member has connections with a program of interest, that can be an added bonus because such ties can be very helpful.

Even if the school does not request it, be sure to enclose a copy of your resume. It should be clear, concise, and accurate, and it should emphasize your strengths. It should also be neat, easy to read, and professional in appearance, either typed or printed on a computer. Your adviser may be able to help with this important assignment by furnishing sample resumes or referring you to any of several fine references for use in preparing a resume.

A word to Canadian students: You may encounter some resistance to applying for residencies in the United States, primarily because of the difficulty of comparing Canadian and United States applicants due to differences in their educational systems. You can overcome this somewhat by including as much information as possible about your training, grades, honors, and so forth. Before submitting your application and support materials, find out if the program will even consider Canadian applicants.

Interviews

Once applications have been submitted, you should be hearing from the programs applied for. Bear in mind that the later in the season that you schedule the interview, the better off you will be. There are two reasons for this. First, the screening process for prospective applicants tends to be tougher in the beginning. With the passage of time, the process tends to get somewhat more relaxed as the program directors get a more realistic handle on the current pool of applicants and their backgrounds. Second, interviewers tend to remember best those they reviewed last when they decide on who is to get the residencies.

Again, as was true of interviewing for medical school, try to group your residency interviews according to section of the country. It works out much better in terms of cost and time allocations. Also, it's a good idea to have a few interviews under your belt before you try for the really big ones—those that you have ranked at the top of your list. This way you can perfect your interviewing technique somewhat before going after your top preference residencies.

Okay, you've applied for residencies in about a dozen programs and nearly half have invited you for interviews. What next? There are several tasks you should take care of before going on an interview that can help to stack the odds in your favor.

First, research the school so that you have a pretty good idea of its clinical and academic facilities and faculty; then list the questions you want answered.

Second, read the literature on your specialty. This way you can be up-to-date on the field, including the type of students being sought and the personal attributes desired—leadership, community involvement, research, or clinical abilities.

Then review your application and support materials to make sure you can answer any questions that may arise concerning your background and record.

Schedule your interview at a time when you can attend morning rounds or a teaching conference. If possible, stay an extra day to talk to residents, especially those from your school. Quite often they can enlighten you as to the strengths and weaknesses of the program that you could not learn of in any other way.

Keep in mind that the interview could lead to a salary-paying job, so take it seriously. Make sure that you are dressed conservatively in a suit (for both men and women). Men should wear a simple white or blue shirt and a neat tie. Avoid loud colors or flashing rings, watches, or jewelry that might distract from the serious business at hand. Sweaters and casual slacks might be okay for times when you are on call, but they will hardly do for an interview. You are interviewing for a professional position, and you should dress the part.

As to the actual interview, here are a few pointers to keep in mind. First, and most important, be on time. Your interviewer's time is very valuable, as is your own; a late arrival does not make a very good impression and is seldom, if ever, excusable. Arrive in plenty of time, even if you have to sit around for a half hour or more—better to come early that to be late.

Make sure you get the name or names of those doing the interviewing, with the proper spelling. Usually you can get this from the department secretary just before the interview. Ordinarily, you will see only one interviewer, but you may be interviewed by several key people in the program. Look them all in the eye when you enter and greet each (assuming that there are more than one) by name and with a firm handclasp. Wait until all are seated (it's only common courtesy) before you sit down.

Keep your priorities straight. Questions about salaries, benefits, and other job perks are perfectly legitimate, but should come toward the end of the interview, after you have a chance to discuss other important aspects of the program.

It may be impossible to get the answers to every question that you have during the interview, but here are a few of the more commonly asked questions that you may well want to consider:

- Is the faculty stable—that is, what is the turnover of faculty? This is a fairly sensitive area, but a very important one nevertheless. Be careful when asking about this and if need be, back off.

- How much contact do you have with the faculty—that is, how often are they in the clinics, wards, or operating rooms where you can have some contact with them?

- Is the program accredited? If not, you will be ineligible to take the specialty board exams and will almost always have to scratch this program from your list of possibilities.

- Where are the graduates practicing? What kinds of jobs are they handling? How have they fared on the specialty board exams? (This is an excellent tip-off on the value of the program.) Does the program help graduates to obtain jobs?

- How much autonomy do residents have in patient care? How much contact do they have with patients? How many patients are ordinarily cared for by residents?

- What requirements are there, other than clinical, in such areas as research and special projects; writing of case reports, reviews, and abstracts; and administration? Such activities can help or they may detract from your clinical training, depending upon your goals, but it pays to get the facts about them ahead of time.

Other legitimate questions include: What changes, if any, in the curriculum do you anticipate? How many hospitals participate in the program? Is there time to attend conferences and meetings? What do residents like most and least about the program? What is the patient mix—that is, how many are private; how many are on Medicare or Medicaid; how many are admitted for surgery or for medical conditions, accidents, or emergencies? And by all means ask about benefits offered—life and health insurance for both you and your family, if pertinent; vacation time; sick days; and maternity leave.

It would also be advisable to get an idea of the number of women residents, the number of married residents, and social activities, if any.

Also find out how often you have call (very important), what happens if you become sick, and precisely what is expected of house staff.

From the program's perspective there are a number of questions that you may be called on to answer, such as the following:

- Why did you choose this specialty?
- What are your goals?
- What are your strengths and weaknesses?
- What schools have you applied to?
- Are you interested in clinical medicine or in teaching or research?
- What can you contribute to this program?

These are just a few of the questions that are commonly asked. Other questions that are not asked so frequently include:

- What are your hobbies and interests?
- What kind of a person are you?

Questions in this category are often intended to try to get to know you better and may seem far removed from medicine. But interviewers may want to see how you handle these, so be prepared for such seemingly far-removed questions.

Some questions may seem tricky, but they really are designed to see how you answer under pressure: What trends do you foresee for medicine in the next decade or so? What problems do you see arising in this specialty in the near future? What happens if you don't match in this specialty? (This is asked to see if you have the foresight to have contingencies in the event this does happen.) Tell me about yourself. (Answer this by being honest and brief and not too detailed.) If further information is sought, let the interviewer follow up on this.

You get the picture. Almost nothing is sacred in the interview, so do the best you can even with questions that may seem highly irrelevant or personal. They may be designed to see how well you handle yourself in sticky situations.

Some questions may be personal, such as those regarding your family, which are strictly illegal but which nevertheless may be asked, especially if you are a female. How do you handle such questions should they arise? First, you can refuse to answer the question on the grounds that it is illegal. But, unfortunately, this could cost you the job. The second choice is to try to shame the questioner into dropping the question by responding with something like: "Is this question really relevant?" This will give him or her the chance to reconsider and to drop this line of questioning. And the third choice is to answer the question in a somewhat ambiguous manner by saying something like: "I have no plans to have a family while pursuing my residency."

Studies have shown that most program directors select applicants on the basis of those that they figure will do well clinically, without causing too many problems; those who are reliable; those who rank high on the national board exams, have high class rankings, and clinical honors in medical schools; and those who interview well. If you fit into any or all of these categories, you can almost name your ticket in getting a residency.

Making the Match

You have now completed the interview process and gathered information on the various specialties in which you are interested; you are now ready to rank the various programs in order of preference. Likewise they have ranked applicants for their programs in order of priority. There remains one major step: to see if a match can be arranged for both applicant and residency program. To do this, the overwhelming majority of applicants and programs participate in a computerized program called the National Resident Matching Program.

This program considers the top choices of both students and programs and then proceeds to match them by order of preference. Initiated in 1952, it has taken many years to perfect—and it works. In 1992, the latest year for which data are available, more than 15,000 residency positions were filled through the NRMP, otherwise known as the Match.

More than 70 percent of the positions offered through the Match were filled with graduates of U.S. and Canadian schools approved by the Liaison Committee on Medical Education. About 11 percent of available spots were filled by non-LCME approved graduates (foreign medical school graduates). Approximately 20 percent of residency openings, primarily those considered less desirable, were unfilled through the Match.

While the Match is the overwhelming choice of most medical school graduates in finding residencies, it should be noted that currently nine medical specialties and subspecialties run their own separate matching programs for filling specialties: neurology, plastic surgery, ophthalmology, neurosurgery, otolaryngology, radiation oncology, urology, preventive medicine, and nuclear medicine. For information on residencies offered by these specialties, write directly to the specialty society itself at the address listed in Appendix B.

Currently graduates of osteopathic medical schools have no matching program of their own to fill residency openings. Osteopathic students interested in postgraduate training in several specialties approved by the American Osteopathic Association (AOA) participate in their own registration program called the Intern Registration Program. Here students and programs do their own negotiating to see if agreements for specialty training can be worked out during the student's senior year

As to the NRMP itself, it has developed to the point where it can accommodate nearly all participating students by matching them with their top choices in residency training programs. Over the years, more than 57 percent of students participating in the program matched with their top choice, 15 percent with their second choice, and 10 percent with their third choice.

In nearly all first-year programs in family practice, general surgery, internal medicine, obstetrics-gynecology, pediatrics, and pathology, as well as the first-year positions in psychiatry and emergency medicine, you can enter directly with no previous residency training and complete all necessary requirements for that speciality.

A few programs, known as *transitional programs*, offer first-year training in several specialties prior to applying for a second year in a specific specialty. A few programs in anesthesiology, neurology, nuclear medicine, ophthalmology, orthopedic surgery, otolaryngology, physical medicine, and neurological surgery offer a first year in internal medicine and general surgery prior to entering training in their specialties.

The NRMP also offers separate matching programs for residency programs in dermatology and emergency medicine and, in addition, offers a number of fellowship programs that provide training in various subspecialties. These are limited to those who have completed the required training in the various specialties involved. The Medical Specialties Matching Program (MSMP) offers fellowships in the internal medicine subspecialties of cardiology, gastroenterology, and pulmonary diseases; colon and rectal surgery; foot and ankle surgery; general vascular surgery; hand surgery; pediatric ophthalmology; and thoracic surgery.

Medical students who participate in armed forces training programs will be involved in a separate match for residency programs offered by the military.

If you have decided on a specialty, you need to find out if the specialty has its own match outside of the NRMP, if some programs are in the NRMP and some are not, or if all of the programs participate in the NRMP. The NRMP participation form must be signed before the July deadline, at the end of your third year. It must be accompanied by a nonrefundable application fee ($25 in 1992). You can rank ten hospitals on your rank order list; if you want to rank more, you must pay an additional fee for each program ranked.

Canadian students participate in their own matching program—the Canadian Intern Matching Service—or the NRMP, or both. If you decide to match through the CIMS, your name is automatically removed from the list of candidates for the NRMP.

Students from schools approved by the American Osteopathic Association can also participate in the NRMP, but since a match thus obtained does not qualify osteopathic students for licensure in most states, it is best that you check this out in advance to make sure that you have not gone through the Match in vain.

Results of the Match program are released in late March on the same date for all and are binding on both applicants and programs, just as if they had signed contracts for the residency.

Although the vast majority of students seeking residencies find their spots through the NRMP, it is estimated that more than a fifth of residents in training programs did not participate in the Match. These were primarily those who found residencies through match programs sponsored by individual societies not participating in the NRMP.

If you were one of the 6 percent of nearly 15,000 U.S. students who participated in the NRMP and did not match, you need not despair. Your school may be able to help you match up with programs that still have openings. A day or so prior to official notification of the Match results, you will be notified if you have failed to match. You are then free to seek out open residency slots, and for this purpose you will receive a booklet of spots still unfilled. You then have a short amount of time to review these spots, list your preferred choices, and contact these programs by phone.

Since time is running out, you should be able to conclude negotiations right on the telephone. You may have to fax the program director a copy of your transcript, dean's letter, and other support materials, but it should not be necessary to come in for an interview at this stage of the game. In fact, you should be wary of any program that requires such an interview before offering you a contract.

CERTIFICATION AND LICENSURE

From the time you complete your residency and fellowship (training in various subspecialties that follows completion of residency training), it is a short jump to certification as a specialist and then to licensure.

To be certified you must have completed a residency of from two to five years in length, depending on the specialty, and an additional length of training for a subspecialty. You must then pass the board examination before you can be certified in that specific specialty.

For licensure for both D.O.'s and M.D.s, you must first graduate from an accredited medical school, complete the licensing examination, and have participated in an accredited residency/internship training program.

You are now ready to hang out your shingle as a licensed and board certified physician, either as a private practitioner or as a member of a group practice.

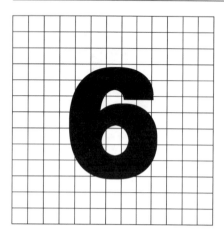

OSTEOPATHIC MEDICINE

Until now, we have confined our remarks to mainstream medicine, often referred to as *allopathic medicine*. But there is another branch of medicine—a small, but nevertheless influential branch—osteopathic medicine.

Doctors of Osteopathy, known as D.O.'s, currently number 37,000 practitioners, about 6 percent of the total physician population in the United States and Canada. But in states where they predominate—Florida, Michigan, Pennsylvania, Ohio, and Texas—they are very influential, as they are in a good many other states. Unlike their M.D. counterparts, D.O.'s tend to practice in primary care areas such as pediatrics, family practice, obstetrics-gynecology, and internal medicine. An estimated 66 percent of all D.O.'s in the United States practice in communities of fewer than 50,000 residents. In many communities D.O.'s are the principal health care providers. Nearly 40 percent are specialists. They are certified to practice in approximately 20 medical specialties as compared with 65 percent of all M.D.'s who specialize.

Even though their training and the training period involved—four years—are similar, D.O.'s are not M.D.'s. They are graduates of colleges of osteopathic medicine, of which there are sixteen in the United States. There are none as yet in Canada, where the profession has not been formally organized.

Neither are D.O.'s chiropractors, bone specialists, or podiatrists, all of whom are more limited in their powers in the areas of treatment and diagnosis.

Like their M.D. colleagues, osteopathic physicians are fully licensed in fifty states to practice medicine in all of its branches; prescribe drugs; admit patients to hospitals, both allopathic and osteopathic; perform surgery; and use all of the commonly accepted forms of therapy, including diet, physical and occupational therapy, and radiation.

DIFFERENCES BETWEEN D.O.'S AND M.D.'S

Even so, there are differences in outlook and approach to medicine between the two branches. D.O.'s, for instance, emphasize the interdependence of all body systems, including the musculoskeletal system, and they believe that unbalances in one body system can cause changes in function in others.

Osteopathic medicine places greater emphasis on *holistic medicine*, which spells out further the interdependence of the body's organs and systems. D.O.'s bring a unique hands-on approach to medicine and view spinal manipulation and palpation (touch) as vital tools in the diagnosis and treatment of disease.

D.O.'s further emphasize the body's natural tendency to stay healthy and its capacity to heal itself. Therefore, osteopathic medicine strives to assist, support, and sometimes to spark the body's innate tendencies to maintain its own health.

Finally, osteopathy, in line with its holistic or body interdependence emphasis, places greater importance on preventive medicine, proper nutrition, and staying fit.

BECOMING A D.O.

Like allopathic medicine, osteopathic medicine requires that candidates for medical school have a bachelor of science or bachelor of arts degree. The required courses are very similar to those of allopathic medicine—usually one year each of English, biological sciences, physics, general chemistry, and organic chemistry. A few schools also require courses in genetics, math, and psychology.

In addition, while most future D.O.'s major in science, chemistry, or biology, they may major in any area, including the humanities, as long as they can meet the minimum course requirements, get good grades, and demonstrate good credentials in science in the MCAT. Finally, just as is the case in medical schools that train M.D.'s, osteopathic colleges require a personal interview to determine your social and interpersonal skills and to see if you have the necessary motivation to excel in the very long and grueling curriculum that leads to a medical degree.

The resemblance does not end there, since the academic program in both colleges of osteopathic medicine and in colleges of allopathic medicine is about the same. The first two years—or basic science years—stress anatomy, physiology, biochemistry, microbiology, pathology, and pharmacology.

As in the training of M.D.'s, osteopathic medicine stresses clinical subjects—those involving treatment of patients—in the last two years of medical school. Included are such subjects as medicine, pediatrics, obstetrics and gynecology, radiation, and surgery, and revolving clerkships through each subject area are featured in the student's third year, the same as in allopathic medicine.

Interspersed throughout the four-year medical program are courses stressing osteopathic principles and techniques. Following graduation, you are then required to serve an AOA approved internship of twelve months. From there, as is true of many M.D.'s, you can go on to a medical residency program in various specialties requiring anywhere from two to five years of additional training.

Before you can practice, D.O.'s, like M.D.'s, must obtain a license from the state licensing board. Boards vary in their composition. Some are made up entirely of D.O.'s, and some of M.D.'s only, while others are composed of a combination of the two.

Requirements for licensure for both D.O.'s and M.D.'s are about the same in all states and grant osteopathic physicians full practice rights as physicians.

Once in practice, D.O.'s can be admitted to any of about 195 osteopathic hospitals located in twenty-eight states, and increasingly D.O.'s are being admitted to M.D.-controlled hospitals as well.

Since the federal government, state governments, and private and public health agencies consider osteopathic medicine as a separate but equal branch of medicine, D.O.'s have all the rights and professional standing of their M.D. associates, and many have been admitted to M.D.-controlled state, local, and national medical societies.

Osteopathic physicians also serve as commissioned officers in all branches of the armed forces. They may serve as medical officers in the civil service, U.S. Public Health Service, and the Department of Veteran Affairs.

WHY REMAIN SEPARATE?

With so many points of similarity, you may well ask why osteopathic medicine maintains its own superstructure—professional organizations, including the American Osteopathic Association—separate but equal medical schools, separate but equal osteopathic hospitals, specialty societies, certifying boards, and so forth. Wouldn't it make sense to merge the two branches of medicine together into one united medical body?

Osteopathy's answer to this question is this:

By combining unique osteopathic principles with traditional diagnostic and treatment procedures, D.O.'s offer a special system of health care aimed at preventing and curing disease.

By treating the whole person, not just the disease, the D.O. seeks to improve the quality of care for each patient. The profession also points to the rapid strides osteopathic medicine has made in recent years. The number of D.O.'s has gone from 13,000 in 1969 to 30,000 in 1991 and to approximately 37,000 today. With this increase in numbers has come increased public acceptance of osteopathic physicians as well. Although osteopathic medicine works together with allopathic medicine in seeking to upgrade the standards of health care in the United States, it does have its own approach and prefers to stay a separate but equal branch of medicine.

THE BEGINNING OF OSTEOPATHY

How did osteopathy reach its present preeminent status in medicine? To trace its origins, we must go back to 1874, to the Missouri frontier town of Kirksville.

There Dr. Andrew Still, a courageous and determined M.D., was becoming increasingly dissatisfied with nineteenth-century mainstream medicine. He was disenchanted with the very rudimentary drugs and surgery then available to treat disease, especially after losing three of his own children. At the time, in the 1870s, anesthesia, sterile surgery, and antiseptics were unknown on the frontier, and X-rays and antibiotics were not even imagined.

To combat the inadequacies of the medicine that surrounded him, Dr. Still founded his own unique brand of medicine, which harkened back to the philosophy of Hippocrates, who is often called the father of medicine. The central focus of Dr. Still's new system was the unity of the body. As the primary feature in maintaining and enhancing body health, he identified the musculoskeletal system, which he emphasized as a key aspect of his approach—a concept that is receiving widespread acceptance in mainstream medicine today.

To make his new approach to medicine more acceptable and to make for more effective medical treatment, Dr. Still stressed palpation and human touch. And he offered spinal manipulation as a less intrusive form of diagnosis and therapy—a concept that has been increasingly embraced by the American public. Today osteopathic medicine offers the full gamut of medical diagnosis and treatment. But it should be noted that the individual osteopathic practitioner has the option of using spinal manipulation or not, according to his or her own dictates.

HOW OSTEOPATHY WORKS

To see how osteopathy works, let's look at a few typical medical cases and how they would be treated by the osteopathic physician.

For example, the surgical removal of a diseased gallbladder is accepted practice by all physicians, M.D. as well as D.O. But D.O.'s believe that medicine should do more than merely repair, remove, or relieve the diseased organ. To the D.O. the gallbladder does not function independently; its nerve and blood supply are also involved as are the chemical balance of body fluids. So besides treating the critical stage of the disease, the D.O. is concerned basically with returning the patient to full health by treating the internal and external conditions that caused the disease in the first place.

This is not to say that the M.D. is not concerned with the underlying causes of disease, but it is simply that in osteopathic medicine, students are trained and schooled to be on the lookout for such underlying causes of disease.

Or take the D.O.'s array of treatments for the correction and elimination of disease. As has been noted above, the osteopathic physician uses the same therapies as does the M.D. physician for the diagnosis, treatment, and prevention of diseases, including drugs and diet, surgery, radiation, and occupational and physical therapy, among others.

But the D.O. has one method that is unique. It may take the form of palpation as a diagnostic procedure to detect soft tissue changes or structural defects in the body; at other times it is seen as a form of corrective manipulation to relieve dysfunction or limited motion of joints. Since musculoskeletal dysfunctions can mimic other disease symptoms, osteopathic manipulation can contribute greatly to the diagnosis and treatment or correction of structural problems.

For example, it is a known fact that diseases of specific organs can produce pain in remote areas of the body. Stomach ulcers, for instance, can cause areas of spinal pain just below the shoulders in the back. Or the spread of pain to the loin from a diseased kidney is yet another example, as is the radiation of pain to the left shoulder a symptom of heart disease. D.O.'s are trained to recognize that symptoms can be mimicked in these other organs to which the pain has been transferred.

Consider also that it is a known fact that disorders of the upper spinal column can cause recurrent headaches. So, if you properly apply manipulative treatment, especially to the neck and head, quite often you can relieve the headache symptoms. This is a small example of how osteopathic medicine, through the holistic theory, strives to maintain peak health in all body systems.

THE FUTURE OF OSTEOPATHY

As to the future of the profession, while nothing is certain, the signs for continued growth and prosperity for individual D.O.'s are brighter, if anything, than for medicine as a whole. Longer life spans and the correspondingly greater need for health care, as well as emphasis on insurance and federally funded programs to pay for the cost of medical care, all point to a greater need for physicians. The greatest need will be for primary care physicians—general practitioners, internists, pediatricians, and obstetrician-gynecologists. Since most osteopathic physicians fall into the category of primary care, the outlook for continued demand for D.O. services is bright indeed.

In addition, the fact that D.O.'s for the most part prefer to practice in smaller communities, where the demand for medical care is the greatest, is yet another reason why the profession is expected to continue to grow in the next decade.

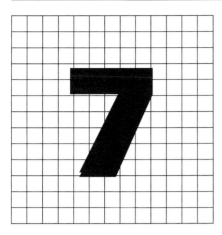

GETTING STARTED AND MOVING AHEAD

Now that you've got your license and medical school diploma in hand and have passed the board for certification in your specialty, you're ready to practice, right? Wrong. You've still got another very important decision to make: whether to strike out on your own or take a salaried position, even if temporary, with an HMO, group practice, or other organization. There are several options that you have in starting a practice and that is what we'll discuss in this chapter.

TAKING A PAID POSITION

First, let's take a look at the pros and cons of taking a paid position or launching your own solo practice. According to the AMA, an estimated 65.7 percent of all new physicians choose to go the salary route, that is, they choose to work for somebody else. And when you examine this closely, you will see where there are many good reasons for this. For one, it takes a lot of courage to strike out on your own. It may require many long months until your practice takes root. Chances are that you will already be deeply in debt for your medical school training, with postmedical school debt now approaching, in many cases, $100,000 or more. That's a heavy load, and for that reason alone many students choose the safe route and take a job as part of a group or working for an HMO, a surgicenter, hospital emergency room, staff position, or other paying position. Then, too, the already deeply burdened would-be solo practitioner faces further debt in trying to raise the capital required to purchase equipment and furniture, sign a lease, order supplies, and pay for all the other expenses that he or she will face in organizing a new practice. In other words a substantial investment of perhaps many thousands of dollars is involved in getting started in a solo practice. Still, as will be seen later in this chapter, many licensed physicians are going into solo practice and there are many good reasons for this.

But there are many other factors involved that put the brake on starting a new practice. For one, a new practice is a gamble and is subject to such outside forces as recession, inflation, unemployment, governmental restrictions, and the economy in general. Personal factors, such as health, energy, and skill in patient and community relations and family problems, can also strongly affect the success of a practice.

Beyond these uncertainties, there are many other problems stacked against starting a new practice for the new physician: longer hours than colleagues in group practices or those who are salaried, less certainty of time off for vacations, difficulty in arranging coverage when you are on vacation or ill, and the need to meet overhead expenses (the cost of keeping the office going, including such expenses as insurance, telephone, electricity, secretarial wages, and so forth, that must be paid whether or not you are working).

The salaried position offers relief from all of this potential aggravation and frustration. Salaried physicians can hold positions in government agencies (federal, state, or local) private industrial and commercial companies, insurance companies, the services (army, navy, air force, and marines), and many other agencies. But perhaps the greatest number of openings for physicians, accounting for roughly 20 percent, are to be found in private hospitals where physicians are in great demand to staff the emergency room or act as consultant or support person in such departments as occupational or pulmonary medicine, and many others.

The benefits of such employment are obvious: good security, attractive benefit packages—paid vacations and holidays, sick days, health care coverage (medical and dental as well, not only for the doctor but for his or her family)—the opportunity to practice in a pleasant setting with congenial associates, the latest in medical equipment at hand, and, last but not least, a good salary (although chances are you could do better in solo practice).

In opting for a salaried position, you avoid all of the headaches and realize many benefits that you might otherwise not have. Health care coverage, for example, is something that you as a solo practitioner would have to pay for and obtain on your own, either by joining a group, an HMO, or some other kind of insurance provider, the same as everyone else.

But there is a price to pay in taking a salaried job that must be taken into account. For one, in accepting a paid position you give up a good part of your autonomy and professional independence. You are now subject to the whims, needs, and desires of your superiors. You are just a part of the team and have limited, if any, say in the way the team is operated.

Also, loss of income is a factor to be considered. Then there is the ever-present possibility of personality conflicts with higher ups, associates, and with patients to whom you may be assigned, which can be very frustrating. But it should be noted that you would still face many of these frustrations even if you practice alone, especially those involving patient hangups and problems.

On the other hand, as a paid employee you work shorter hours than your self-employed counterpart, and have a much better handle on your time off—vacations, holidays, and days off.

Although taking a salaried position is undoubtedly the preferred route of many starting physicians, the fact is that in just a few years, the situation changes dramatically. According to the AMA, the number of employed physicians dropped sharply from 65.7 percent during the first two years of practice to 32.4 percent with six to eight years of practice, and to only 27.5 percent for those with nine to eleven years of practice behind them. These are overall figures. The number of salaried physicians varies a lot by specialty, ranging from 100 percent of pathologists with two or fewer years of practice to 83 percent of radiologists with similar experience and dipping to 42.5 percent for psychiatrists and 51 percent for general surgeons.

Another big consideration is the fact that women are much more likely to opt for salaried positions than men. Although the percentage of women opting for employment was only slightly higher in the first two years of experience, the decline was not nearly as sharp with more experience as it was for men. In the most experienced category (those with nineteen or more years of practice), women were more than twice as likely to be salaried than men (35 percent as opposed to 17 percent).

LAUNCHING A SOLO PRACTICE

Solo practitioners, though not nearly the force they once were in the profession, are nevertheless still a force to be reckoned with, accounting for more than 60 percent of all physicians currently practicing. Any way you look at it, that is not a number to be sneered at. What exactly is a solo practitioner? Donald M. Donahugh in his book, *Practice Management for Physicians*, puts it this way: "A solo practitioner is one who has a direct relationship with each patient. He provides professional services to the patient, is personally responsible for that care and receives a fee in exchange for his services."

What is the appeal for having your own practice? As we have seen there are several factors, including greater autonomy and independence. But beyond that there is the opportunity to establish long-lasting and highly satisfying relationships with your patients. There is also, of course, the possibility of losing a patient (you can't win them all), but for most practitioners the former is much more likely than the latter.

As a solo physician, you are much more independent than your salaried colleagues. You can choose your location, the office layout and design, color scheme, size, fees, personnel—just about everything having to do with the practice. For better or worse you are in charge, and if things go right, fine. But if not, you have no one to blame but yourself, or perhaps the economy. Ordinarily, however, after several lean years, during which you are building the practice, you will peak to the highest salaries of all physicians with comparable experience and backgrounds.

We have already cited some of the problems of solo practice, such as long hours and difficulties in arranging coverage if you should take ill or need a vacation. But there is also the relative isolation of most solo practitioners to consider. Ordinarily, you have no one to consult with regarding the best treatment or diagnosis for your patients. Most likely you will have no business manager to handle the thousand-and-one forms required by the government at all levels, by private pay insurance carriers, by patients, and so forth. It is a never-ending and often seemingly losing battle to keep up with all of the paperwork.

Many old-time private practitioners are calling for a return to the days when the physician had more control of the practice. Today he or she is increasingly backstopped by the federal and state governments in such programs as Medicare and Medicaid and by third-party payers (insurance carriers) to make sure that all treatments and tests are warranted and that hospitalizations do not exceed a given number of days for any given diagnosis. But the nature of solo practice and the very fact that so many doctors are still in their own practices would indicate that solo practice still has a lot going for it.

WORKING IN A GROUP PRACTICE

The second most popular form of medical practice, accounting for more than 40 percent of all physicians, is group practice, which has been growing like wildfire in recent years. For instance, in 1965 there were 4,289 groups covering some 28,000 physicians, while in 1991 there were 16,500 groups accounting for more than 184,300 physicians, a more than 400 percent increase in about thirty years.

The AMA defines a group practice as "the application of medical service by three or more physicians formally organized to provide medical care, consultation, diagnosis or treatment, through the joint use of equipment and personnel with income from the medical practice distributed in accordance with methods previously agreed upon by members of the group."

Although this in general defines a group practice, the precise nature of the group—how members are to be admitted, how revenues are to be distributed, and how expenses and various other considerations will be handled will vary from group to group.

In general, a group may be an association of solo practitioners, a corporation, or a partnership. But more than two-thirds of all group practices are incorporated, while the vast bulk of solo practices are not. There is a reason for this, since the primary reason for incorporation is that all assets and expenses of the group are part of the corporation. If a member of the group should be sued for malpractice, the corporation as a whole cannot be sued, and its assets cannot be touched if he or she should lose.

In the case of the solo physician, since he or she and the corporation are one, to all intents and purposes, there is no valid reason to incorporate as would be true for the group.

Why the big movement to group practices in recent years? There are many reasons. Since group practice often represents a pooling of revenues and expenses of all of the members of the group, outlays for equipment, technical services, and facilities can be taken from revenues and are often superior to what is available to the solo doctor. Utilization is often better as well, since if certain members of the group have more patients than they can handle, it is often possible to assign new patients to other group members, particularly the newest physicians to join, who may not be so busy.

Coverage for vacations, weekends, and illness is more easily arranged since vacations and other time off is assigned to all members in turn on a regularly scheduled basis. Such coverage does not depend upon a volunteer. Since coverage is assured, individual members can better plan their vacations and days off.

Then, too, members of the group as a rule work fewer hours per week than do solo doctors, and the hours are more regular. In the larger groups (five or more members), income is only slightly lower, if at all, than would be the case for a self-employed physician.

There are still other advantages such as the greater availability of office personnel to take care of the increasing number of ancillary services such as blood drawing, blood pressure taking, and so forth. Also, the group can hire a business manager experienced in personnel, office operations, and bookkeeping to fill out the myriad forms required and to supervise all business phases of the practice, a luxury few, if any, solo physicians enjoy.

In response to this, solo practitioners point to the greater independence they have, in terms of not being bound by group practices and restrictions that may not be to their liking. Also the group practitioner is subject to disagreements with other members of the practice, which can be annoying and frustrating.

Finally, as a member of a group, you are not only more restricted in your practice options but in possible income as well, since you are limited in the number of patients seen, hours when you can see them, and so forth.

These are the main options that you have in going into medical practice. But there are several other options that also should be considered.

OTHER PRACTICE OPTIONS

The first, a variation of solo practice, involves becoming associated with an older and more experienced physician who is seeking to cut down on his or her practice and hours worked and eventually, perhaps, sell the practice.

Such an association is attractive to both you as the physician seeking to become established and to the older physician as well. For the younger physician, it is a good way to become established in the community. As the senior physician introduces you around the community, you immediately form relationships with community residents. And you have the opportunity to learn firsthand the business aspects of running a practice without having to be fully responsible for any mistakes that you might make.

The senior associate benefits by being able to cut down a little on the workload and hours, and at the same time lower costs.

In such an arrangement, it should be clear to all concerned that this is a relationship of convenience and that senior and junior physicians have solo practices and merely wish to share expenses. Nevertheless, such an association leads in nearly all cases to a more formal arrangement if the participants are compatible. Although such an arrangement may not be bound by a legal contract, it is best that specifics of the association be spelled out by a written document or memorandum of understanding signed by both associates.

Quite often such an arrangement can develop into a partnership between the two principals. In this case a legally binding document spelling out specific details of the arrangement—including such things as lease, equipment, personnel salaries, and apportionment of utilities and telephone—should be signed.

A very real possibility for you as a young physician is the purchase of the practice through such an association. An acquired practice nearly always offers a good location that is completely equipped. In many cases the selling physician will act as a consultant both as to the patients and the handling of the business side of the practice. Of course, here it is essential that the doctor purchasing the practice know how to evaluate the practice correctly. This involves reviewing such factors as gross earnings, assets, lease, improvements, and goodwill, all of which are discussed in Dr. Donahugh's book, noted above. This is an excellent resource on learning what to consider in evaluating an established practice.

WORKING FOR HMOS

Still another option is becoming affiliated with a managed-care type of health program such as an HMO (health maintenance organization), PPO (Preferred Provider Organization), or an IPA (Independent Practitioners' Association). Here you have the option of signing on as a salaried physician in an HMO or merely participating in a managed-care program as an independent practitioner or a member of a group. HMOs, or managed-care programs, are sweeping the country, and estimates predict 100 million members by the year 2000, with the current number of people enrolled surpassing 50 million. What's more, as many as 77 percent of all practicing physicians are participating in managed-care programs of one sort or another.

Basically there are three types of HMOs. The first is patterned after the progenitor of all HMOs, the Kaiser Permanente Plan and the Health Insurance Plan of Greater New York. Under this arrangement, the doctors involved are partners of the group and the success or failure of the group is reflected directly in their success or failure.

The second category is the staff arrangement, where doctors involved are on staff and are salaried employees. Doctors do not participate in any distribution of profits nor are they involved if the HMO fails to show a profit for any given year.

Under the third arrangement, doctors are part of a group practice known as an Independent Practitioners' Association (IPA). Here participants are loosely affiliated in the HMO and work on a part-time basis. For most partners in such an arrangement, the HMO supplies roughly 10 percent of their patients.

Since the greatest part of their practice is outside of the bounds of the HMO, the doctors involved do not rely on the success of the plan. It is merely a supplement to their basic practice.

Whatever type of arrangement you decide upon in starting your practice—salaried group, partnership, junior associate with a more senior physician, and so forth—the details of the arrangement must be clearly spelled out in a letter of agreement or a contract to avoid misunderstandings.

HOURS AND INCOME

Other considerations are involved in starting out in practice. Hours, for instance, vary according to practice. A recent AMA survey showed that salaried physicians worked 57.5 hours per week as compared with 60.3 hours for solo practitioners.

The impact of the type of specialty is seen by the fact that, according to the survey, in 1994 GPs, or family physicians, worked 56.5 hours a week, while internists worked 63.1 hours a week, and radiologists 56.8 hours a week. Pathologists worked the shortest amount of time, logging in 48.2 hours a week.

Likewise, salaries for doctors varied considerably by specialty. An AMA survey showed that primary care physicians in 1993 earned lower salaries than surgeons. Specifically the survey showed that general practitioners/family practitioners averaged $116,800 per year; internists, $180,800 a year; pediatricians, $135,400 per year; and obstetrician-gynecologists, $221,000 per year as compared with surgeons (of all kinds) who averaged $262,700 per year. All salary figures quoted are net (after expenses but before taxes).

But within the broad category of surgeons, earnings of surgery subspecialties were considerably higher in 1995 according to the Medical Group Management Association. Thus neurological surgeons, with eighteen or more years of experience, were averaging $416,000 a year; orthopedic surgeons, $277,000 a year, and cardiovascular surgeons, $527,000 a year.

Although such trends as Resource Based Relative Value Scales (RBRVS) have closed the gap in salary somewhat between primary care practitioners and specialists, there is still no doubt that the gap continues to exist.

FINDING A POSITION

Getting started is yet another consideration. There is little doubt that where doctors do their residency will have a great impact on where they practice. During residency many residents receive offers from the attending staff who are looking for junior partners. Here, of course, the advantage is that the two physicians in joint practice know each other and their capabilities and are well equipped to decide if their years of working together would likely lead to success in a joint practice, either in an association of solo practitioners or in a partnership.

In addition to this possibility, there are the local, state, national, and specialty society journals, which run ads for physicians wanted and carry lists of new graduates seeking positions. New physicians seeking positions should by all means check out any opening by traveling to the area where the opening is located and discussing the position in person with the physician or physicians involved, before making any kind of a commitment.

Physicians in a partnership work together very closely and though work habits, temperaments, and personalities may differ considerably, they may not show up until some time has gone by. Or two physicians in a partnership may have widely varying capabilities in treating patients, and the one seeing considerably more patients per session may feel shortchanged if he or she is sharing equally in the partnership.

Besides the professional journals and medical societies, there are medical employment agencies that can help you find a position.

If you are thinking about starting your own practice, you might well consider taking a part-time medical position to help tide you over until your practice requires your full attention and energy. For example, you may be able to find part-time employment in clinics that pay so much per session, or in hospital outpatient departments or emergency rooms where you may be able to find work during evening hours or on weekends.

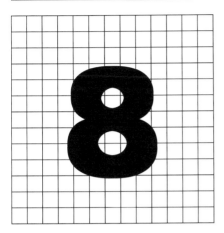

A LOOK AT THE FUTURE

Trying to predict the future of medicine is like trying to walk on shifting sands. There have been so many changes in medicine that if physicians practicing around the turn of the century were to be transported Rip Van Winkle–style to the offices of today's practitioner, they would scarcely be able to believe their eyes.

From essentially a profession of solo practitioners, where 90 percent of the doctors had their own practices, medicine has gone to one where group practices, partnerships, and salaried physicians, as we have seen in the previous chapter, are making their presence known in increasingly greater numbers.

The composition of the profession has likewise changed with vastly increasing numbers of women being attracted to medicine as practitioners, teachers, and researchers. In 1969–70 women accounted for only 9 percent of first-year medical students. By 1979–80 they comprised 29 percent of all first-year students, and today they number better than 40 percent of all first-year medical students.

Ironically, though the number of women joining the profession has risen sharply, the number of applications from men, which had been rising sharply before women started applying for medical school in droves in 1969–70, has dropped sharply. Since 1974–75, when applications from male students peaked at 35,000, the number of male applicants has dropped steeply to about 18,000, a decline of roughly 50 percent.

Even stranger, perhaps, is that despite warnings by many of an oversupply of physicians by the year 2000, record numbers of students are applying to medical school. The 16,000 bright young medical students who started school in the fall of 1994 were selected from a pool of applicants more than three times that number, according to Dr. Gary Krieger in an article appearing in *American Medical News* in October 1994.

Krieger claimed that the chances of filling a medical school opening are so slim that some students applied to as many as forty medical schools in hopes of landing maybe a half dozen interviews and one acceptance.

And all of this is happening at a time when there is considerable discussion of an oversupply of doctors. According to Dr. M. Roy Schwartz, AMA group vice president of medical education and sciences, by 2010 the United States will have 163,000 more doctors than it needs.

And the Council on Graduate Medical Education, a body established by Congress, foresees a surplus of 115,000 specialists but a shortage of 35,000 primary care physicians by the year 2000.

Quibbling aside, most experts agree that prospects are most promising for doctors that go into primary care, such as family practice, internal medicine, pediatrics, and obstetrics-gynecology, and not so good for many specialists.

Several articles in such publications as the *Wall Street Journal* and the *New York Times* have reported ominous stories of recent graduates of specialty residencies being unable to find jobs.

Despite this, many contend that the profession is not suffering from an oversupply of physicians but rather a maldistribution—that there are too many physicians practicing in the large metropolitan areas of 500,000 or more and too few in the smaller communities of 50,000 or fewer.

What this all means as to the future of the profession is at best murky, but there is little doubt that salaried jobs for physicians, already on the increase, will accelerate. And there will be an increase in primary care physicians— those in internal medicine, family practice, obstetrics-gynecology, and psychiatry. This will be accelerated by the entrance in increasing numbers into the profession of women, since women have tended to practice in salaried jobs and in primary care specialties much more so than men.

Recent decades have also seen a growth in group practices, with ever-increasing numbers of doctors opting for salaried positions. It is believed by many that because of efficiencies involved in group practices and through managed care, such as HMOs, fewer physicians will be able to care for more patients, and this in turn should somewhat limit the need for more physicians.

However, predicting medical manpower needs can be tricky. For instance, with the recent decline in the number of births, one might be able to extrapolate that there would be a need for fewer pediatricians, but as the saying goes, it ain't necessarily so.

Likewise in cardiology, one of the most overcrowded of the specialties, according to the Graduate Medical Education National Advisory Committee, will the increased use of such diagnostic tests as cardiac catheterization, the procedure which allows the physician to tell by X-ray the extent and location of arterial blockage, require more cardiologists trained in this procedure? And how will such new procedures affect cardiovascular surgeons, who are trained in such procedures as bypass surgery?

CLOSING THE REIMBURSEMENT GAP

What will be the effect of such new developments as the Resource Based Relative Value Scale (RBRVS), which has been introduced by the federal government on Medicare payments. This new system, which is required of third-party payers, reimburses practitioners on a new scale taking into account such factors as time invested in a patient, cost of training the doctor, and cost of the practice.

As has been seen in the past, insurance companies, and the government, too, in such programs as Medicare and Medicaid, tended to pay a premium for the so-called doing procedures, exemplified by many areas of surgery, while the cognitive skills of primary care physicians were often disregarded.

Will the new emphasis of RBRVS tend to iron out the previous inequities in reimbursement and thus make primary care more attractive for students?

Nobody really knows. And what about Physician Diagnostic Related Groups. If this proposed system is launched, this could further lower the income of many specialists. Under this system, an extension of the current DRG plan providing the basis for hospital reimbursement under Medicare, various diseases and diagnoses would be lumped together, and the physician, instead of being reimbursed on a fee for service basis, would be paid a fixed amount regardless of the time that he or she has invested in the patient or any unforeseen complications that might arise. This form of reimbursement, also known as prospective payment, is here now for hospitals and is believed to be on the horizon for physicians.

ESCALATING HEALTH CARE COSTS

Further influencing the need for physicians is the unparalleled rise in the cost of health care. For several decades health care has been skyrocketing, and the end is nowhere in sight.

In 1993 Americans spent more than $884 billion on health care, roughly 11 percent of the gross national product. Health care is by far the fastest growing component of the GNP, far outstripping food, shelter, and transportation. If present trends continue, the cost of health care will triple by the year 2000 and account for nearly 16 percent of the GNP. Even at the present 10 percent of the GNP, cost of health care has had an impact on other aspects of living—food, transportation, shelter, and so forth.

The reasons for this explosion in health care usage are many and complex. For one, there has been a tremendous acceleration in population growth. Thanks to medical science and technology, people are living longer and are better able to withstand the ravages of diseases that not too long ago would most likely have resulted in death or disability. Such diseases include polio, pneumonia, hardening of the arteries, diabetes, and many others.

And this rise in our longevity has been accompanied by an almost proportional demand for medical services. Putting it another way, the longer you live, the more vulnerable you become to potentially fatal or crippling disease.

But beyond medical technology, it's a fact that vast numbers of people are now covered by insurance—both private and public. Only a few decades ago, the bulk of Americans, estimated at 90 percent, paid for medical and health care services out of their own pockets. Today the government (through Medicare and Medicaid and other federally sponsored health programs) and private insurance programs, including HMOs, foot more than 50 percent of the health care bill, thus making health care available to millions of Americans. Just a few decades ago many of us would have hesitated to see a doctor or even go to a hospital; today we think nothing of doing both since they are covered and paid for, or at least partially paid for, by a third party.

Accompanying this expansion of coverage has been a tremendous upsurge in our awareness of health care services, including medical treatment, through the greater publicity being given health care in the media. Today it is not so unusual to see or hear reporters that specialize in medicine and health care on the radio or TV or in newspapers and magazines. Add to this the ever-expanding demand for services and the tremendous costs associated with developing new products, procedures, and drugs, which can reach millions and multimillions of dollars, and you get some idea of why health care costs have shown such a steep climb upward. Whatever the reason, there is little doubt that the costs of health care, medical services included, have gotten out of control.

Government Efforts to Curb Costs

As the largest health care payer, accounting for nearly 43 percent of the health care dollar, the government has in recent years taken steps to put the brakes on health care costs. We have already seen the first step in that direction with the imposition of the DRG (Diagnosis Related Groups) system as the basis for payment of hospital bills under Medicare and the strong possibility of extending this to physicians' fees. Accompanying this new payment system has been the establishment of peer review groups to monitor hospital admissions, length of stay of patients, and other activities. This applies not only to Medicare patients, but to those covered by Medicaid (the state-operated health care program for indigent patients) as well.

Business Efforts to Curb Costs

But in a way this is just a small taste of things to come. Big business and industry have gotten into the act as well. With health care costs now in excess of $800 billion a year and costs rising each year, companies have a big stake in attempting to control spiraling health care costs.

In fact, by not taking action, companies could see their profits wiped out within the next few years if health care costs continue to rise. Consequently many companies have hired doctors to check the validity of employee health care claims. They also are requiring second opinions. Some are increasing outpatient coverage in an effort to reduce hospital stays and providing incentives for employees to be cautious with the health care dollar.

But there is more. The sixties saw big business, in the form of not-for-profit holding corporations, enter health care with a vengeance. It started in the field of nursing homes and has become so involved with them today that it is estimated that more than 50 percent of all nursing homes are owned by vast health care conglomerates or corporations.

The seventies marked the entrance of for-profit businesses into the hospital field. Through cost efficiencies and better screening of patients, they have in many cases been able to flourish and show profits, while many of the smaller nonprofit hospitals have increasingly felt the pinch and have gone out of business. This trend has accelerated in recent years.

There has also been a trend on the part of many, if not most, hospitals to acquire nursing homes, rehabilitation centers, surgicenters, or ambulatory care centers, sometimes in direct competition with doctors.

In addition, physicians are feeling the pinch of competition stemming from other health professionals—nutritionists, stress counselors, and especially chiropractors, all of whom provide alternatives to the more traditional kinds of medical care. Chiropractors, though unable to prescribe medicine or perform surgery, can treat patients in their own manner. Currently chiropractic has seen a quadrupling of graduates in the last decade, and as a group their median age is thirty-seven. What's more, chiropractors are now covered by Medicare and Medicaid, so more competition can be expected from that quarter.

WHAT'S TO COME

So out of this welter of varying trends and forces affecting medicine, where do we stand? We see factors that would seem to create a demand for physicians, and others that would seem to lessen this demand.

Under such circumstances, predicting medical personnel needs for the next twenty years is tricky indeed. But the medical specialties that are expected to grow and show a surplus of personnel in the next few decades are, according to the AMA, those in the primary care areas: family and general practice, internal medicine, pediatrics, obstetrics-gynecology, and geriatrics. Those expected to show surpluses are cardiology, gastroenterology, and anesthesiology. Much smaller increases in personnel requirements are foreseen for surgical subspecialties, psychiatry, pathology, and surgery.

It should be noted that Congress passed legislation in 1963 expanding the size and number of medical schools, in response to an anticipated severe shortage in the number of physicians. As a result, the number of M.D.-dominated medical schools went from 89 to the present 124 and osteopathic medical schools went from 8 to 16, respectively. This enabled medical schools to nearly double the number of graduates turned out by 1980 and likewise to double the number of doctors in practice. As noted in Chapter 1, the number of applicants per medical school spot dropped from 2.8 in the mid-1970s to 1.6 in 1988 but rose again to 2.6 in 1994–95, with women comprising 42 percent of the application pool. The Council on Graduate Medical Education sees a surplus of 115,000 specialists, which includes those in cardiology, gastroenterology, infectious diseases, endocrinology, pulmonary medicine, and several others.

It should be noted that even with the predictions of surpluses in certain areas of medicine there are literally thousands of communities across the United States and Canada that are very underserved as far as doctors are concerned. In many smaller communities there are no physicians at all, and residents may have to travel dozens of miles to reach the closest physician.

It is primarily for its willingness to serve the needs of small town, rural areas that osteopathic medicine has registered such great gains in both membership and influence in recent years. It is for this very willingness to go where the needs are greatest that the future looks so bright for osteopathic medicine. And it is likewise for this very unwillingness to settle in smaller communities that some observers have criticized the main M.D.-dominated branch of the profession.

Others have attached their hopes of correcting current imbalances in both pay structures and numbers to such a system as the RBRVS. As Walter Benjamin commented in an editorial in the *New England Journal of Medicine*, "finesse of scalpel, catheter and CT scan is not superior, but complementary to the diagnostic and pharmacological brilliance of the generalist. One form of medical artistry is learned by standing for hours at the surgical table; another form, learned from experience."

When some members of the profession earn $500,000 and more a year, while primary care doctors may make only $100,000 with the same amount of schooling, residency, and experience, clearly something is wrong.

Benjamin also criticizes the profession for creating a situation in which 25 percent of all practitioners list some form of surgery as their specialty but only 8 percent are in general or family practice. His solution is the immediate enactment of RBRVS to help iron out these differences.

SOME CONVERSATIONS WITH MEDICAL PROFESSIONALS

This chapter contains the highlights of some taped conversations held with professionals and students involved in medicine. Ideally it will give you a clearer perspective on what is involved in pursuing a medical career.

FRESHMAN MEDICAL STUDENT AT A PRIVATE COLLEGE

I did my undergraduate work here as well as my medical training. I'm from the Washington, DC area—Falls Church, VA.

For me the decision to go into medicine was a very gradual one. I did not know from the minute that I was born that I was going to be a doctor. It developed a lot in high school where I had a very influential biology teacher. I learned from him that you didn't necessarily have to just go to class and regurgitate everything that you had learned. I learned from him something about thinking about problems and how to approach what you were learning.

He was interested in theater and so was I, and he was also my director at one point. So from him I developed an interest in science and the humanities and the thought processes used in analyzing what you do in the humanities and the arts.

I went to a private high school in DC and they emphasized that kind of thinking. I always thought that science was separate from the humanities. I always thought of myself as an arts person. In fact my classmates in high school are flabbergasted that I'm going into medicine. I try to explain to them that the kind of skills that you use in medicine are actually a kind of analytical skill, and that makes much more sense to them.

In college a lot of my courses emphasized that same sort of thinking process. I took theoretical courses which emphasized designing experiments and the experimental aspects of science. And that sort of whetted my appetite for science and math. A lot of my friends were pre-meds and we shared a lot of the same values. So everything started to come together and all of a sudden I decided medicine was a great way for me to combine my interest in science and my interest in humanities.

In choosing a medical school, I applied actually to twenty-two schools primarily because there was a discrepancy between my MCAT and my grades. Where I had extremely high grades, my MCAT scores were horrible—they were just average. I had the foresight to realize that could cause some problems, and it did. It led to many rejections. The first school that offered to interview me accepted me very early on in the processing. But when I was accepted here, I withdrew from that school, which was of somewhat lesser caliber. I could have gone to school in Virginia, which of course was closer to home and financially more attractive. However, I considered the values that had been imparted to me as an undergraduate would prove useful in my medical education as well.

I got a very well-rounded education here, and even now in med school there's a real emphasis on trying to experience all aspects of medicine, not only the clinical stuff, but also getting some research experience and getting some experience in ethics and really try to make a broad, well-rounded physician.

As to med school itself, volumewise it's been much tougher than I expected. It's not only the work but the amount of time we have to spend in lab, classes . . . it's a lot.

Conceptually, it's not much harder than undergrad. Unfortunately, the first year of medical school is getting the basic sciences, and a lot of that is just rote memory and that's not the reason I went into medicine. That's been sort of difficult because of the problem of seeing how this all relates to clinical aspects of medicine, but we have had some exposure to patients. We have had a clinical skills course—actually a significant amount of time in the hospital where we were all required to do two patient interviews with residents and we then break into small groups with a resident and an intern and each week we take turns doing interviews. And we'd break into small groups and psychiatrists would really evaluate us doing patient interviews. Every week we'd visit the hospital two times, once with the residents and once with the psychiatrists. That was last quarter.

This quarter we aren't in the hospital, but we're working on writing up patient histories. They bring in doctors from the hospital, have them interview patients, and then we're expected to synthesize the data and write it up in a form that would be acceptable.

And this seems to be par for getting exposure to patients during your basic science years. I've spoken to friends in other schools and they have had similar experiences—in fact even less clinical exposure than we have had. In many cases they have had patient exposure in a large classroom setting, but not in a small group, like we do.

As to the future, I have an interest in primary care and generally in pediatrics. I'm also thinking of going into child adolescent psychiatry or possible a dual program in pediatrics and child adolescent psychiatry. But definitely something in the field of pediatrics and much more of a patient approach than, say, like doing pediatric neurosurgery.

As to my day, a typical day would be this: we start class at 8:30 A.M. and usually we're finished by 4:00 P.M. and this includes about an hour for lunch and maybe a half hour break. That includes all lecture classes and lab.

And then it depends. Some weeks we're lucky and we only have lab three days a week; other weeks it's four times a week. Like today, we got out for the first time this week around 1:00 P.M., so that was a real early day.

In terms of studying generally what I do is, after I get out of lab, I go home, have dinner and maybe if I feel up to it go swimming or to the gym or do something on that order for a little bit. Then by around 6:30 P.M. or 7:00 P.M.–7:30 P.M. at the latest, I go to the library and am usually there till about 1:00 A.M. That's my daily routine. That's pretty typical. I see the same people at the library every night, so I know that I'm not the only one.

I'm at the library a lot on weekends, too. It depends. Some weeks—like last week—we had three tests, so I spent the whole weekend studying for those tests. If there's no test involved next week, generally what I try to do is take Friday or Saturday night off and then I'll spend a decent amount of time studying on Sunday. It's rare that I'll have the entire weekend for myself.

I give swim lessons on Saturday morning so I know that I'm always going to do something a little different at that time. I do that to make a little extra spending money, but also because I enjoy swimming and I enjoy working with the kids. Besides swimming I really like musical theater. I'm not really a performer but I love to catch the latest musicals downtown or any theater. I just saw *A Midsummer Night's Dream*. I also enjoy dining out and am taking commercial aviation. I don't have a pilot's license, but I enjoy flying. The whole thing fascinates me. At one time in college I was thinking of going into the arts, which was a very strong interest of mine.

I don't know if I would want to practice in a smaller community or not—that's something I would like to explore. This holds true of research, as well. I've only done a little research and would like to do more over the summer, if possible.

The university is encouraging us to do research over the summer, and I've applied to several research programs. I've also applied to several fellowship programs that are rural oriented. I'm going to have to see what pans out this summer, but am looking forward to experiencing some research or working in a rural medical environment to see how these register with me. When I came here, I thought they would pressure me into doing some research, since they are so research-academically oriented, but that has not been the case. They are encouraging us to do research this summer, and I am exploring several options in various medical fields.

Scholastically, I'm doing well. We're on a Pass-Fail system so it's pretty hard not to be doing well.

Perhaps the most surprising thing about medical school, I have found, was the diversity of my classes. I had no clue as to what it would be like. From undergrad work, I had a pretty good feeling of what medical school would be like and that it would be pretty intense. But I have found my class to be quite surprising and the students are quite diverse—from all sorts of backgrounds having all sorts of interests and having done many different things before even coming to medical school.

The future of medicine will see a much different kind of practice. I think people in my class have not such a high expectation of the materialistic and they have more understanding of ethical issues and current topical issues in medicine, and it's been interesting seeing what this new breed of physician/student is like.

Finally, I would advise students who are considering medicine as a career that they should not be disturbed by the need to take organic or basic chemistry or physics. Medicine may be a science, but it's also a huge art. I have friends who were thinking of medicine as a career who were turned off by the science requirements. Sure, you must have some science, but it's not nearly as rigorous or demanding as many students think. And you don't have to be a physics, chem, or bio major to get into medical school. Many people in my class majored in English or the humanities, and they are doing quite well. It's really too bad that these science requirements are used to weed out people. They are only part of the curriculum and should be no problem if you really want to go into medicine.

THIRD-YEAR MEDICAL STUDENT

I decided on medicine as a career because by nature I am very inquisitive and want to take care of people. There are no others in my family involved with medicine in any way.

I liked biology, and what better way to apply biology than through medicine. Medicine is very exciting. What we learn now will probably be obsolete in three years.

There is no question that I have made the right decision. There's nothing else that I would rather be doing. I could probably be doing other things, but don't want to. Most people here are bright enough to be engineers or physicists if they wanted to, but I wanted only medicine from the start.

I applied to about twenty schools and was accepted here and by a few other name schools. I ended up here for personal reasons. I was engaged at the time, and my ex-fiancée was involved in physical therapy at a large hospital here in the city. Chicago was the city in which she wanted to be, and I wanted to be affiliated with a top-notch school, which was the reason I decided to come here.

In undergraduate work, to prepare for medicine, I took a lot of science—physiology, organism biology—and did teaching as an undergrad. I also worked on autopsies in pathology for the first two years of undergraduate work and did volunteer work on the outside, all geared toward medicine.

In the third year of medical school you have to decide on what area of medicine you want to practice—pediatrics, internal medicine, ob-gyne, surgery, or whatever. Then should you decide to go into internal medicine, for instance, you can wait for a couple of years of your residency before deciding on which subspecialty of medicine you want to enter.

As to medical school itself, the first two years, I, like a lot of us, asked myself what I was doing here. Why do I care about this, especially in this school, which is one of the nation's leaders in research? In the first two years of school, you deal with a lot of minutia which, quite frankly, has very little if any clinical implications at all.

The entire third year is clinical and much more enjoyable, because then your studies are more applied. You forget things that aren't important and learn things that are. The first two years of school were not relevant for me, but the clinical stuff was wonderful.

Medical schools are all experimenting with changing curriculums. Harvard, for instance, has eliminated all formal first-year studies and elected to base everything on case studies, so everybody talks about someone with diabetes for a week, and then perhaps they will concentrate on something else, be it arthritis, or whatever. It is definitely clinical in approach and does away with a lot of minutia that is irrelevant. Even here they are adding courses in psychiatry and in psychology and a course in nutrition—classes which over the years have been lacking.

Are doctors remote and hard to talk to? Perhaps. The biggest complaint that we get is that doctors are remote and not into caring about their patients. I think that this has a lot to do with our personality. At this medical school, we care a lot about our patients, but I am not certain of how good we are at showing this. Personally, I feel that I do pretty well in relating to patients. I feel humble, and my patients seem to relate well to me.

There seems to be some reluctance on the part of the doctors about letting third-year medical students take care of patients, and I still run into this attitude even now.

My specialty—cardiology—involves a four-year residency after completing a residency in internal medicine. I am sort of in a special category because I am getting through medical school courtesy of the air force. For the three years of school that I have completed, I will have to put in three years of work in the air force. You must agree to serve in the air force for a year for every year of schooling that you receive. And, in return, besides covering your medical school costs and tuition, they pay you a stipend of $700 a month.

At the end of my fourth year, I'll be going into air force medicine if they want me to do a residency, and I'll have to do it. There are contingents of medical students in the army, navy, and air force, and Washington has become very competitive with kids from all over the country wishing to serve the various branches of the armed forces.

If I had my druthers, in the long term I would like to work out of a university clinic. My specialty would be cardiology, and I would like to practice right here in the Midwest, or possibly in the Northwest, where I met my wife.

If I had to do it over again, there are several things I would do differently. I think that as an undergrad I would have taken less science and more humanities—possibly more Shakespeare, who is one of my favorites. You have almost no time in medical school for outside reading, but a lot of schools are looking for individuals who are more well-rounded.

Eventually, I intend to go into teaching. As to medicine itself, I find it to be a very helpful and exciting career. The first two years were rough. But now, while I am still tired, I am more convinced than ever that this is the right career for me. The third year of medical school is easier, just like I understand that the first year of a residency is hell and that it gets progressively easier as you go along. I also understand that the MCAT (Medical College Aptitude Test) has been completely revamped, and that there will be less and less emphasis on biology and chemistry. They are also revamping the state boards, which you must have for certification to practice medicine.

SECOND-YEAR RESIDENT IN REHABILITATION MEDICINE

I was born and raised in New York City and did my undergraduate work at Dartmouth College and medical school at UCLA. I did my first-year residency in internal medicine here at the University of Washington in Seattle, where I have three more years to go to complete my residency. I am single.

I decided on medicine because I was good in science in high school and gravitated toward medicine as a career when I was a freshman in college. I took political science and languages and went to China on one of my trips after finishing college. There I studied the Chinese language and was teaching English to Chinese doctors, and that once again got me interested in medicine. So when I returned to the states, I thought about trying medicine again and enrolled at Bryn Mawr College, which has a baccalaureate premedical program for those who have finished college but need premedical credit to get into medical school. I did fairly well after completing a year there and worked for a year in a hospital as a researcher and as a pulmonary function technician at Columbia University. From there I went to medical school at UCLA.

I like medicine because, for one, I find it very intellectually challenging and, second, because you feel like you are really helping people. You feel like you are doing the right thing for people. It's rigorous, but you feel like you are accomplishing a lot. Ultimately, I may wind up in academics, but I should know better what I will do after finishing my residency, and if I will go into private practice or research.

Today more and more physiatrists, which is what specialists in physical medicine are called, are working in outpatient facilities as opposed to inpatient care, mainly because it leads to a more controllable life-style. Also because that's the way medicine is going in general—toward more outpatient care. Probably more physiatrists have mixed practices, consisting of patients seen in both outpatient and inpatient facilities. That's the nice thing about medicine. You can do almost anything that you want.

Originally, I was interested in neurology, but neurology is more attuned toward diagnosis rather than treatment. Physical medicine is really about a patient's quality of life, making decisions and changing the way they live, and that to me is the ultimate goal in medicine and where I would like to focus my energies, rather than in looking into the intricacies of someone's biochemistry in terms of their liver function test, or how their heart is doing. To me what is really important in general is what type of limitations their illnesses place upon them and what they can do to limit their problems.

I chose the University of Washington for my residency because they have one of the best programs in the country in physical medicine. It's a four-year program—one year of internal medicine and three of physical medicine.

In choosing a specialty, there are several considerations. First, do what interests you—that's what you should go for. It's silly to choose a specialty based on the amount of money you would make or the amount of free time that you would have. Having said that, I think that life-style is very important. If you want to have a family and want some control of your free time, you won't be able to be a neurosurgeon, which has gotten to the point where it is almost all-consuming. Physical medicine can be a very hard residency, but nowhere near as time consuming as others.

Secondly, it does not necessarily deal with acute medicine, where you deal with patients that are acutely ill, so that you are not always being called to handle life-and-death situations. So if you want to have some control over your personal life, it's an excellent field.

In considering a career in medicine, it's very important to spend some time in a hospital and to talk to a lot of doctors, to find out what doctors do. Medicine is a field that offers tremendous opportunities. It's a lifelong intellectual challenge. People who are interested in making money are not necessarily the best doctors. You make good money in medicine, but can make more doing other things and have more time.

Regarding residences, I found that I adjusted to it better than I thought I would. They tell you that the internship year (the first year of your residency) is going to be the worst year of your life—and it is.

VETERAN UROLOGIST AND ASSOCIATE PROFESSOR OF UROLOGY AT A LARGE PRIVATE MEDICAL SCHOOL

In college I took a lot of Asiatic language studies with the intention of going into this field some time in the future. This was at a small college near Hartford, Connecticut. I took a year off between college and medical school to establish residency in Colorado.

I then went to the University of Colorado in Boulder and finished there in 1980, and from there I went to Tufts New England Medical Center in Boston, where I did two years of general surgery.

At that time in most of the surgical subspecialties, you had to do at least two years of general surgery. And then I took a year and went to France, to the American Hospital in Paris, where I was chief resident of medicine and surgery. Then I returned to the States to do four more years of training at Harvard in urology.

How did I get into medicine? Well, that's quite a story. Neither of my parents went to college, but my Dad's brothers all went to Harvard. And one of my great-uncles was a very famous doctor. He was the first doctor to actually diagnose FDR with polio, and he was one of the consulting physicians for President Eisenhower when he had his heart attack, so he was a very big man in medicine.

I probably saw him about six times in all, mostly when I was a little child because he had passed away before my Bar Mitzvah. So I don't remember him very well, but he had a great influence on me because my family spoke of him often and he was enormously respected. Then, too, one of my Dad's brothers was also a very well-known Harvard cardiologist. And so when I was in my early teens, I had already decided that medicine was something of great appeal to me.

I decided to go into urology somewhat through the process of elimination. Nowadays, there is a very definite push to put medical students into primary kinds of practices. But when I was in medical school that was just starting to happen. At the University of Colorado, they had a strong family practice program. I enjoyed every field of medicine that I took during my four years of medical school. Each segment was interesting to me—pediatrics, general internal medicine, cardiology, surgery, and even psychiatry appealed. But as I got closer to the time when I had to make a decision, I realized that what seemed to be most interesting to me was surgery. And I liked urology because it had the broadest opportunity to see patients of every age with a very broad spectrum of disease, from kidney stones to cancer, fertility problems, and so forth.

It also was challenging in that I would be responsible for making the diagnosis. In many cases, surgeons have the patient presented to them by the internist, all ready to go—perhaps the patient has a gallbladder problem, and all the surgeon has to do is take it out. Or the patient has a heart problem—so fix it. In urology, you are more responsible for your own diagnosis, and this presented more of an intellectual challenge to me.

And in urology you have more association with patients than most surgeons. And then, too, I think many of the problems in urology were not altogether worked out. The way I feel with regards to surgery is that surgery is a primitive therapy for a complex disease. As we get better with our diagnosis and better with our treatment, we're going to find fewer and fewer surgeries necessary. It's already happening. When I started out in urology in the eighties, one of the biggest areas of concern was kidney stone disease. Now we have this lithotripter that crumbles the stones mechanically and thus enables the body to get rid of them. And so, in some areas we have made great progress, and as we get to understand the disease better, we can use less invasive, less injurious approaches in our treatment of disease.

As to my family and personal life, I'm married and have two daughters. There are several ways of looking at how medicine has affected my personal relationship with my family. If you look at it one way—it has compromised my personal life enormously. I don't have the same kind of daily interactions with my daughters as my friends. I have two daughters—ten and seven. I'm at best home for dinner once a week. And three out of four weekends a month, I'm in the office. Besides my clinical duties, I write for various medical journals and do research. So this consumes what little time I have left when I am not taking care of patients.

But from my viewpoint as a physician, I find that I have no choice. It's what I want to do and for me to be best in my clinical practice so as to be able to make a contribution to medical science and to get my own personal satisfaction. To get those kinds of things, which are clearly important to me, this is a sacrifice that I have made.

I put in somewhere between sixty to eighty hours a week in my professional activities. Whatever free time I have, I am reading my journals, if not writing articles for them. And I attend between three to five major medical meetings a year. And in three out of the five, I'll be presenting papers as well as attending.

After finishing my training, I spent five years at the University of Chicago Medical Center where I was assistant professor of surgery and director of education for the department of surgery—including all surgery and surgery subspecialties.

And here at Rush I am associate professor of urology and I am co-director of education for the department of urology. I am also involved in our residency program, where we train about three or four young doctors a year. We are responsible for all training, including teaching during surgery and giving a regular lecture series. Here we work more on a clinical basis rather than in the classroom, and we are more involved with the care of patients.

There are some things that bother me about the way medicine is evolving in our society today. In a way I think that society and medicine itself has killed the golden goose so to speak. We have right now the finest medical care and treatment programs in the world. Everyone in the world of medicine looks to the United States for answers. We are the guiding light in medicine. But because of third-party payers and Medicare, which has opened up the Pandora's box of medical care, and which enables people to get care for nothing—they have no investment in their care. But as a result of this, costs have skyrocketed, and this great rise in the demand for medical care is the primary cause for the rising costs of medical care. And because of the lack of attention of physicians to what's happening, we now have nonphysician trained people dictating what can and cannot be done in patient care and treatment. Some of this is good and most of it is bad. What we will see in years to come in this country is a change in attitude of physicians.

The majority of young doctors coming out of school may be in debt $50,000–$100,000. And if they have no expectation of having a reasonable income, based on their education, this will undoubtedly have some effect on the quality of those who go into medicine. Unfortunately, in this world, money happens to be somewhat of an incentive to work. It's very easy for the young physician or the young person going to medical school to say that I want to dedicate my life to science, to education, and to serving others. But there was a sense that they would be rewarded for it, that they would be appropriately paid, that their children would be able to go to college, and that they could count on having a nice vacation once a year. And I believe that that era is probably over.

Also, as a result of managed care, doctors have less control over what should be done for their patients and instead are restricted in their activities by decisions that are based on cost, which is compromising care. And this tends to reduce the investment that the physician has in offering care.

In summation then, if sciences turn you on, if service to people turns you on, if you like the intimacy and privilege of being able to take care of people—that is something that turns you on—then you should by all means consider a medical career. The idea of making it rich, being in a sense a very powerful person in the community—this status is rapidly changing today. If you are interested in the complexity of medical problems, then this is something that you should do. The other thing that's fascinating about medicine is that almost everything becomes routine in life, but in medicine, in a sense, you are always on a learning course. If you thrive on that idea of learning all the time, then medicine will be a very satisfying life-style.

PROFESSOR OF MEDICINE AND DIRECTOR OF CLINICAL PHARMACOLOGY

First of all, I should say that I didn't intend to go into clinical pharmacology. It was such a new discipline, and programs were generally not available in this area when I was in medical school.

I had always been interested in chemistry and physiology, and pharmacology in particular. As a senior medical student, I had taken elective research work in pharmacology, although I didn't have a clearly formed idea of even doing research at the time. I finished Cornell University Medical School in 1993 and have a degree in chemistry from Harvard, where I did my undergraduate work.

I went two years into house staff training internship and residency at Massachusetts General Hospital during Vietnam and had to do my military service before I could continue house staff training, so I went to the National Institutes of Health for two years during the war. And it was there that I became interested in clinical research, while at the National Institute for Allergy and Infectious Disease. There I worked on a number of infectious diseases including leprosystemic mycoses (fungal diseases). It was there I began doing what is now recognized as clinical pharmacology—during the years 1965–67.

After another year of medical training, I came to Northwestern as chief medical resident in 1968. People at Northwestern suggested that I get more training in clinical pharmacology and then asked me to start the program there in 1970.

It is now a medical subspecialty, and there are several areas of concentration. You can do drug abuse and drug testing, or you can focus on therapeutic drugs and drug therapy for patients, and finally, you can do a tertiary care specialty for a research and teaching center.

Here in medical school, I run the drug assay lab for the hospital and for physicians, advising them on drug therapeutic problems. So, aside from patient research, I don't do primary clinical practice.

Obviously, if physicians ask me a question, I am available to help them. For instance, take a patient who is having trouble with the anticonvulsant drug dilantin, which can cause problems, and the physician often wonders why the patient is not recovering as well as expected. The blood level recorded may seem unusual in view of the dosage prescribed, so I might be asked to advise them on that. I would then give the patient a special test to see if there is something going on or how the drug is binding to proteins in the patient's blood.

When I started here there were no labs of this type in American hospitals. Mine was the first lab ever set up to apply research chemical techniques to the daily care of patients, and this has really developed over the past twenty-one years. I also function as the hospital quality-control person and chair the pharmacy and the drug therapeutics departments, which decide about drugs to be carried in the patient pharmacy, as well as a committee that investigates adverse events that may occur on patients.

When working at the National Institute of Health in clinical pharmacology, I was doing what today would be called clinical pharmacology, but at the time was thought of merely as infectious diseases. I was encouraged by the fact that my training as an undergraduate student in mathematics, chemistry, and physics could be applied to help patients and answer what I thought were clinically important problems.

My particular field is understaffed throughout the country. Not every medical school has a program in clinical pharmacology. Out of the present 122 medical schools, probably only 30 to 40 have programs even in name—there are only about ten medical schools that have training programs in clinical pharmacology, which are funded by NIH, so that anyone finishing the program can have various job opportunities in academic medicine or in the pharmaceutical industry. Or even with the government. In the FDA (Food and Drug Administration), the agency needs people desperately with this kind of training.

We might be called on to work with a company to look at a new drug, or sometimes we are interested in certain drugs. We've actually gone to companies, and there is a breakdown product of protein or existing drugs, so we have actually initiated studies both in animals and humans of that particular drug.

We might consider hiring a company to look at the new drugs on the market, or sometimes we are interested in certain specific drugs. So we have actually initiated studies in this area.

In my work, I may refer to the mathematics of how drugs are distributed in the body and how they are eliminated. I probably spend about half of my time on research and about a quarter in teaching. I teach about 10 percent of the second-year students a course in pharmacology, and about a quarter of my time is spent on administrative work.

The department includes four faculty members besides myself. Most have had special training beyond that of the conventional specialty—be that obstetrics, cardiology, or oncology, but they have a secondary specialty in clinical pharmacology.

One of our doctors, for example, is training in ob-gyne and in clinical pharmacology. Recently she was in the news for her efforts on a low-birth-weight baby. She was part of a team who made the baby's birth possible. Her major research specialty is the optimization of drug therapy in pregnant women.

Many pregnant women have asthma and have to take theophylline, for instance. Our doctor has become expert in the changes that occur in pregnancy that would necessitate a change in the drug dose for such women.

Generally, the residents who do best in our program have had undergraduate training in chemistry and will have at least two years of calculus. Some may even have an engineering background in college, but must be really interested in research. All too often we find that many young people have good ideas for research but lack the stick-to-itiveness that is required and are unwilling to apply themselves to come up with an answer.

Beyond the chemistry and calculus, we do not necessarily require an M.D. degree. We have, for instance, in our department a Ph.D./biochemist who is expert in analytic and synthetic chemistry. It just doesn't make any sense to apply mathematics to drug therapy if you don't have good measurements of the drug or if you don't know what compounds are being converted to in the body—so we need that kind of expertise as well.

It's a subspecialty—could be either of internal medicine or anesthesiology, or could even be a subspecialty of psychiatry. The man binding element is that researchers have a special interest in using drugs scientifically.

This year we are offering our first certifying examination in clinical pharmacology, and requirements are that you must have had training in a primary subspecialty and additional training in clinical pharmacology. You can then get a certificate of competence. If you are a Ph.D., you could have training in primary care and two years of clinical pharmacology, so you could do it in five years altogether beyond medical school.

With regard to large drug companies like Abbott or Searle, most often I would function as a consultant to them. There are also several drug companies that will send their staff to sit in for a month or six weeks in an advanced course that we teach every fall in this area. So, I am not doing any actual work for drug companies but am advising them as to how to set up their respective programs in clinical pharmacology.

In the future, I believe that what is happening in the automobile industry in quality control will be happening in medicine as well. And the clinical pharmacologist is in the best position to help monitor the quality of drug usage. I have been chairing a committee for the Joint Commission on the Accreditation of Healthcare Organizations, which certifies about 4,500 hospitals and health care organizations every year in a program that is called the "Design for Living." Through this program, the Joint Commission is trying to improve the quality of drug utilization in health care organizations—that is, by using the right drug at the right time and in the right dosage. Many of the things that have been part of the research techniques in clinical pharmacology are such a part of the expectations for optimum clinical care that they are being woven into the fabric of day-to-day patient care.

There is an opportunity for the clinical pharmacologist to play a leadership role in trying to develop ways to monitor usage—developing so-called indicators or guidelines which the Joint Commission can review as the basis for determining if the hospital is using drugs effectively.

ATTENDING ANESTHESIOLOGIST AND DIRECTOR OF OBSTETRICAL ANESTHESIA

Prior to joining the staff at Illinois Masonic Medical Center in Chicago, I was with Michael Reese Medical Center from 1972 to 1974 as an attending anesthesiologist and director of obstetrical anesthesia and had a teaching appointment to the University of Chicago.

I did two years of my residency at Northwestern and one at the University of Illinois. Anesthesiology now involves a continuing training program of four years, including the first year or internship year, followed by three years of anesthesia training. The first year can be a broadly based internship clinical in orientation—no straight radiology or pathology or psychology, but it could be in the fields of internal medicine, ob-gyne, surgery, or peds (pediatrics), or a mixture like the old rotating internships.

I did my medical school training at the University of Illinois in Chicago. I became interested in medicine largely as the result of my high school biology course and through the study of anatomy and physiology and zoology—that was the biggest reason for my choice of medicine, a choice made when I was fifteen, and working in a drugstore after school, which whetted my appetite.

At one time I even considered being a pharmacist, which was somewhat related to medicine, but changed my mind. I got interested in anesthesiology during the first year—internship—in internal medicine doing a rotation in anesthesiology, which seemed to offer experience in dealing with acute medicine and also seeing the immediate results of drugs and their responses.

This is a very open field for qualified students, and there is not the backlog of applications in the field that you see in various surgical specialties, many of which are hard to get into such as ophthalmology, ENT (ear-nose-throat), neurosurgery, and plastic surgery.

I also am very much involved in training students [he is also a clinical professor of anesthesiology] and hold various other positions in the department, such as training anesthesia residents in a program approved by the ACGME (Accrediting Council for Graduate Medical Education), which is a branch of the AMA and the AAMC. With approved free-standing residencies here, I hold various positions: one as chair of the resident selection committee and chair of the clinical competence committee, which evaluates residents. I am also a member of the curriculum committee, vice-chairman of the department, director of quality assurance, and of the medical school committee, which includes the senior medical school electives subcommittee. Committee work never seems to stop; neither does my work in medical societies and in anesthesia societies.

Anesthesiology is somewhat unique in that teaching and clinical work in resident-teaching programs are the same. I may be supervising one of two rooms in the operating room. If there is an anesthesia obstetrics case scheduled, there will be another attending to relieve me, and then I would cover the anesthesia-ob case with a resident-in-training. So almost all of the time I am working, I am also teaching. On-the-job training is really clinical teaching. Right in the operating room, things are happening as medical students rotate through the department.

We get medical students in one of two ways: those who are going through their clinical rotations in the third year of medical school and spend a week or two in anesthesiology as if it were part of a surgical subspecialty. Or if they are taking a senior medical student elective in anesthesiology, we get students who are not specifically attached to a surgery clerkship. Usually this type of elective lasts four weeks and is a more intensive experience. The student may not be totally committed to anesthesiology, but feels that it would be a good way to spend four weeks.

As to what it takes to succeed in anesthesiology, in many ways anesthesiology is no different from any other specialty. We look for the same kind of students. It would be good to have bright individuals who score well on exams. They are always welcome. They should also be comfortable in an emergency situation, emotionally mature, and like doing things with their hands. Last but not least, they should be reasonably self-confident. Occasionally we get some who can't fit these standards. Some may leave the field on their own; others have to be dropped. Still others enter through other medical specialties for various reasons. They may not have been happy where they were. Medicine gives you considerable flexibility to change your field on the specialty level. In other words, once you complete the basic training, there is a lot of latitude in medicine, so that you can change your specialty at the postgraduate level. It is possible to get a new lease on life without incurring a lot in terms of years of training invested.

The benefits in anesthesiology are excellent. If you like to see immediate results of what you do rather than have to deal with chronic conditions or if you like to practice acute medicine, acute physiology, and acute pharmacology, where you see immediate changes resulting from what you do, then this is the field for you, as opposed to internal medicine, let's say, where conditions can be chronic and one needs to have a lot more patience and follow patients for weeks and weeks on end before seeing any results.

An advantage and a drawback is that patient contact is limited. Usually you see patients before the anesthetic is administered and after recovery. Most of your contact verbally or with other people is with other personnel or workers. My contact on a daily basis is with other personnel, either in the operating room with surgeons, nurses, and residents, or with medical students. So I deal a lot in collegial relationships with other people who are connected to my work rather than with patients per se, although how one approaches patients and how one talks with them before they are anesthetized is also very important.

One other thing, anesthesiology is traditionally a high-risk profession. When you are a doing kind of doctor, people can get hurt. I am making a distinction between thinking doctors and doing doctors. It's not that there is no cognitive effort involved. There is, but we become more and more procedurally oriented. It's a numbers game, and the more procedures you are involved in, the greater the likelihood of someone getting hurt, or being unhappy about the results of the procedure. Now because of improvement in safety and technology, we are no longer in the highest-risk category. The malpractice insurance carrier now says that the most risky subspecialty in terms of getting sued and in cash payout are such high-risk fields as neurosurgery, obstetrics and gynecology, plastic surgery, and orthopedic surgery. These are the highest-risk specialties in terms of what you must pay for malpractice coverage. According to the American Medical Association, annual malpractice premiums averaged $16,700 per physician in 1995.

The next highest-risk field would be general surgery and vascular surgery, and anesthesiology would be in the next category down. But basically in any field where you do things and where you stick needles in arteries or do such procedures as angiograms, things can happen. Those in cardiology who stick catheters in patients pay much more than those who don't.

As to hours, my twenty-four-hour in-house call happens once a week. This is pretty typical of the entire field, but in academic anesthesiology, we get called less. You could be on call only once in fourteen days in a large teaching medical center—once a month would probably be more typical. As long as you are not working late in the operating room, you are home free. So there is a big advantage in that there are no office obligations after hours. Once you're through with the operating room, usually you will not be bothered with phone calls.

Sometimes anesthesiologists get involved in pain clinics, or non-operating-room duties. If you are involved with pain clinic kinds of patients, you could be a primary care physician for some patients. I know of one prominent anesthesiologist who was originally a surgical resident and who then contracted polio and lost the use of his legs and had to work from a wheelchair. He was then weaned from surgery to anesthesiology, which he was able to handle from a wheelchair, and he became interested in nerve blocking, and he was very prominent in academic anesthesiology. Pain killing is one area where anesthesiologists have gotten away from a passive role in patient care to a more active role like that of the primary care physician. Blocks in the operating room and nerve blocks could be both diagnostic and therapeutic depending on the reason they were given. Some anesthesiologists are also involved in acupuncture and in transcutaneous electrical nerve stimulation. Pain clinics tend to be multimodal in what they offer. They can offer physical therapy and even manipulation. Some of the texts contain a section on manipulation that sounds just like a chiropractor. In other words, they must know what spinal manipulation involves. So pain clinics tend to be much more eclectic. They can involve physical therapy and nerve injections and blocks as well as the aforementioned manipulation.

INTERNIST AND CERTIFIED GERONTOLOGIST

I went to Washington University in St. Louis as an undergraduate and then to Rush Medical College in Chicago for my medical school training. I remained at Rush for my internship and my residency in internal medicine.

In college I majored in psychology with the intention of going into medicine. I was premed from the start. Didn't take science as a major primarily for two reasons, and would recommend this to others. For one, science courses are generally the hardest of all, depending on where you are. In many colleges, biology, chemistry, and organic chemistry are very difficult. But when I was in college, grades were always paramount in being admitted to medical school, and while the schools will say that grades are not the only factor and that they look at your overall background, the fact remains that without the grades you will have a hard time getting into medical school, and if you do have the grades, regardless of extracurricular activities, you have a good shot at getting in. So grades are a big factor that you cannot get around. I suggest that if you concentrate on one science course at a time, you have a much better chance of getting an "A" in that course.

Secondly, it broadens your horizon, because you don't want to be a whiz at science only. It's a good idea to have knowledge in other areas and not be so focused that you have no peripheral vision. Besides, medical schools are looking for people who are well rounded, and who have many other interests besides medicine.

I got into medicine for basically two reasons: For one, in school, biology seemed to be the subject of greatest interest for me. And in high school, I enjoyed working on projects involving the human body. I enjoyed biology and thought it was fun and was fascinated at how the body works. The other factor in choosing medicine was the fact that my father was a physician, so I was exposed to medicine at a very early age, and this was certainly a factor in my choice. But it was not because I really liked some other field and said to myself, "Well, my dad is a doctor and I'll follow him." The fact of the matter is that I always have enjoyed biology, and I have always liked people, so medicine seemed to be a good way of combining these interests.

I always assumed that I would go into private practice like my dad had done, since that was what my exposure had been, and I was not sure I really had a broad enough vision of medicine to really understand all of my options. I probably did not experiment in enough areas to really get a good feeling of what my options were.

As to my choice of internal medicine, a lot of your feeling about this depends upon the people that you work with and who you look up to. If you're in a hospital with a tremendous ob-gyne program and the people are terrific and great teachers, and you really admire them and are enjoying your exposure there, you will lean toward ob-gyne. If internal medicine happens to be the best specialty you have been exposed to, you lean toward it.

The experience obtained in your rotations in your third year of medical school is a big factor, and you should try to get as much experience in these clinical rotations as you can before deciding on the field in which you wish to specialize. You don't have a lot of time, since you must apply for residencies at the beginning of your senior year.

Generally my day has three components—hospital rounds, teaching, and office hours. Over the years my time investment in these areas has fluctuated, and there are other areas that you can get into for diversity. For instance, at first I did not just sit in the office and see patients eight hours a day, five or six days a week, but I became involved in doing consultations for psychiatric patients, working with a substance abuse program at the hospital where I was training. I was one of the few interns in this area, so everyone was calling on me for consults. And I ended up doing this about 30 percent of my time. And I became the medical consultant in helping to make a videotape for continuing medical education on alcoholism. I was also teaching, and through some friends, I was introduced to a real estate developer who builds retirement homes, and I was offered and accepted a chance to become medical director of a few of these homes. This began about eight years ago and lasted until about two years ago and was quite different from my private practice. So there were many different things going on in my career. Because I could not handle all of these various activities very well, I took on an associate to help out, and he did more of the office practice and helped me with consults, and I spent about 20 percent of my time as medical director.

I was still teaching, doing consults, and seeing private patients, which ended up accounting for about 20 percent of my time.

But this all went through an evolution. It's important in medicine that you be flexible because everything is changing—hospitals are opening and closing, primarily closing. There are fewer opportunities, and more people are looking for the chance to do the same thing. So eventually the psychiatric hospital where I was doing all of my consults closed, and the day this happened I lost 20 to 30 percent of my business.

In addition, the fair-housing laws affected greatly the work that I was doing for the retirement homes, and my work in this area was halted. So I was no longer able to screen applicants for these retirement homes to make sure that they were ambulatory and independent because this was considered discriminating against the handicapped. And so we stopped screening, and new management took over the homes, and my involvement in this activity dropped by 70 percent.

This all happened at about the same time several years ago. In addition, my primary hospital changed its affiliation from the University of Illinois to the University of Chicago for the training of medical students and residents. As a result of all of this, I learned that the only security you have is your own private practice, which no one but yourself controls. And I also learned that medicine is a business, and like any business it's difficult when you depend upon others and cannot control your own destiny, so I wound up concentrating on and expanding my own practice.

Unfortunately I lost my associate because I was not around enough until then to expand and build my practice, and he was uncertain of what the future was with me, so when he was offered a good position elsewhere, he took it. We're still friends, and he works out of my office two days a week, but we no longer are associates.

It's unfortunate, but when we go through medical school and college, we focus too much on medicine and science. It would be worthwhile for anyone planning a career in medicine or research to have some sort of business education. Because much as you might not want to think of it that way, running an office or practice or running a health care department is a business, and you get no business experience in medical school. You really should know something about accounting principles, overhead, insurance, personnel relations, unemployment insurance, and matters of this nature, and that's why so few medical school graduates are going into private practice but are joining groups instead. If I had known this, I probably would have done things differently.

Today I allocate my time like this: Teaching is about 16 percent of my time. My practice and hospital rounds account for the balance of my time.

I have a large number of geriatric patients, because working for my dad for a number of years before he retired, I inherited a lot of patients that loved him, so automatically I had a lot of geriatric patients.

Second, the area in which I practice has a high percentage of geriatrics, so many of the new patients I see are also geriatric patients. So I took an examination to become certified in geriatrics as well as in internal medicine. However, I do not list myself as a gerontologist because I really enjoy handling the younger patients in my practice, as well as my geriatric patients, who account of 75 percent of my practice.

Private practice of internal medicine is one of the most difficult options in medicine for two reasons: first, you are basically on call all of the time, especially if you're a solo practitioner and you have responsibility for care twenty-four hours a day. You never know when you will have an emergency which you cannot foresee and schedule, so your patient load is unpredictable. And second, you are expected to be 100 percent accurate and available. And I might add that you are the most underpaid of all of the specialists because internal medicine is a cognitive skill and has never been paid on the level that procedural medicine has been paid. Patients and insurance companies are oriented toward paying for procedures. That is why applications for residencies in internal medicine have dropped 30 percent.

Today's graduates don't go into internal medicine anymore. They go into radiology, anesthesiology, ophthalmology, orthopedic surgery—into fields where they can get paid a lot for a small time investment. When you consider that an eye doctor gets $2,000 for cataract removal, which takes him forty-five minutes to do, and it takes the internist five to six days of work to make that much money—it's not very equitable. So, many who do go into medicine, rather than going into private practice, go into areas involving procedures. Who can blame them? I can sit in my office and make $60 an hour, and someone in a subspecialty can do one procedure for $500 in 20 minutes. And that's why Medicare is now seeking to see how the system works. There always will be a discrepancy in how doctors are paid—procedures will always be paid more than cognitive functions. There will be some narrowing of the gap, but it will not be dramatic and will not catch up and equalize.

As to private practice, today instead of having patients who pay you and write a check at the time of the service, you now must deal with HMOs and PPOs, and you have Medicare, commercial insurance, and every company has their own requirements for payment. Some require that you call the insurance carrier before you hospitalize somebody; you must have authorization. Medicare is supposed to change their entire billing system. Who knows what that will mean. We may even end up with National Health Insurance. So you have the headaches both from the business and the practice sides.

Liability insurance certainly detracts from our profitability. We are constantly making sure that we are covering ourselves. I know a urologist who is also a lawyer. If I send a patient to this doctor, no matter what the problems, the patient will get a complete workup. Most urologists will say that they don't believe it's worth proceeding at this point with all of these tests, but some feel it isn't worth the legal risk.

If I have somebody with a severe headache and don't do a CT scan, on the one hand, I am liable if there's a brain tumor. And, on the other hand, more and more insurance companies won't let you test unless you have a good reason, and a severe headache is not enough of a reason to proceed. So the insurance company, on the one hand, tries to limit testing, and fear of malpractice makes it obligatory. If I have someone in the hospital with a bad heart, I will more often call in a cardiologist now to cover myself. If that patient has a complication, even though the cardiologist has not changed anything that I do, I can say that I have a cardiologist on the case and the cardiologist has agreed that this is what I have to do. So the doctor has a lot of extra expense because of liability. Our insurance premiums go up, and that can account for 15 percent of our income, so it's a constant problem, which goes back to the need to be perfect all of the time and not miss anything, cover yourself, and make sure that you're not liable and cannot be sued for anything.

At the same time there is a lot of positive feedback in medicine when you help save people's lives or make them feel better. There is a lot of gratification in the work. I see people who are commodity brokers, and their net worth in life is based on the numbers on the board at the end of the day. It's the old feeling of "See, I'm better than you because I've made $50,000 and you've only made $30,000." That's why a lot of them get into charity work to make their lives more fulfilling and meaningful. I get fulfillment out of my practice, as well as aggravation.

In summary then, medicine is an excellent career and there are many rewards to be gotten out of it, and we really need bright people to enter the profession. It is particularly rewarding if you enjoy working with people. If you like working with your hands and doing procedures, there's a lot of potential in medicine.

Don't expect to find a lot of financial rewards—don't look at the money as an end in itself, or you'll have trouble. If you want to go to medical school, you must be completely dedicated to it. You will have to work hard on your grades because that is still an important criterion in gaining admission to medical school. It's not the sole criterion for entrance, but it's still very important.

As to how to deal with patients, there's more and more that's coming out in the training. As a matter of fact the American Board of Internal Medicine now requires that you judge doctors on their humanistic qualities and their ability to deal with patients. It's part of a trend in medicine toward more humanization of the field. We now have psychosocial rounds. Last month we had a meeting on interviewing patients and how to tell them about a serious illness.

The AMA has courses in that and we receive brochures on the subject from private companies. This issue is becoming much more important in medicine. Medical students should take some basic courses in management, and they should become more familiar with computers because by the time they enter the field, just about everything will be computerized.

DIRECTOR OF ADMISSIONS AT A PRIVATE MEDICAL SCHOOL

This year we had 8,702 applications and we will interview about 650 of those and accept about 220 for a class of 104 students. We accept more than we have room for because we know that some of those whom we have accepted will register in other schools where they have also been accepted. But of the 8,700 who apply, only about 4,500 complete the application and go through the entire application process.

Incidentally, it should be noted that applying to medical school is not cheap; it will run a student on the average $1,500 to apply to any school including the cost of taking the MCAT and travel to each individual medical school, and then each individual school has an application fee of anywhere between $50 and $100. The National Association of Advisors for the Health Professions has a travel desk plan that will get students the lowest rate available on air fare, but it's still really expensive.

Most of our students will have multiple acceptances and will have applied to twelve to fifteen schools—that's the national average of schools that each student applies to today. It's not so much a matter of going for numbers. You could apply to 100 schools and if they were the wrong schools, you still might not get in.

State residency is a very important factor. So many schools give preference to state residents. Even here in Illinois, all of the medical schools except one, give preference to Illinois students. We accept 40 percent from the state, Northwestern accepts 50 percent, and Rush and Loyola are both over 80 percent Illinois students. And that's true of all of the states.

And then students need to look at the success rates of students from their schools. If a school has not taken a student from your college in over thirty years, then it hardly makes sense to apply to that medical school. Your premed adviser should be able to assist in choosing the right school, and then you can read carefully material about the school. If it says that their average grade point average for acceptance is 3.5 and you have a 3.0, it's kind of silly to pursue applying to that school, unless you can show a reason such as illness in the family or need to go to work, and can show that your grades have been going upward in the last two years.

This year is again a peak year. The expectation is that applications will begin to decrease within the next few years, but at this point we continue to see an increase like never before—this was a record number of applications for us.

There's a lot of discussion about why this record number of applications at a time when medical opportunities in certain fields are actually decreasing. For one, we feel that the pipeline to medicine is very long. It's the eighth graders now who are really beginning to think about careers in medicine. So the students we're talking to now decided to pursue medical careers long ago and are continuing that interest now. They feel that this is the right choice for them and they have not been dissuaded by the press coverage of medicine's future. They're very excited about the future of medicine, eager to be a part of it, and see themselves as pioneering a new way to deliver health care.

I might point out that it's not just the students with top scholastic records that we accept. That would be an easy job if all we were interested in were just the numbers.

In evaluating the backgrounds of students, we take into consideration their scholastic grade point average, their MCAT, and their motivation—they are all pieces of the puzzle and must all be there. They have to be able to show that they can academically manage the demands of medical school, they have to show that they can handle it interpersonally, and they have to demonstrate that they know why they want to go to medical school. If any of these pieces is missing, then they're not a candidate for admission.

We are seeing more students who are interested in entering primary care, but we see that less here because our mission is not to produce primary care physicians, but a good percentage of our students will be primary care doctors. In the future I am sure that students will be exposed to clinical settings where they can see more families and have an opportunity to work with families over a period of time.

In terms of the increased number of applicants, there are people applying now who did not really have that option before. One large group is women. There are more women applicants now than ever before.

Here we accept about 48 to 52 percent women, and this is fairly typical of what's happening in all medical schools.

Students who see a professional career as the way to security are choosing medicine in much larger numbers. Fewer students are choosing law school, fewer business school or engineering, but more of them are choosing medicine.

And I see students who have a greater commitment to service than in previous years—even five years ago. There are more students who are going into medicine because it's the way that they want to serve their fellow men. They seem to have more of the luxury of being more idealistic. It's an exciting trend.

And we are working very hard to increase the number of students from underrepresented backgrounds. We regularly talk to high school groups. We do all we can to help increase that representation in our student body. Last year we were about 3 percent underrepresented minorities—primarily African-Americans but also including mainland Puerto Ricans, native Americans, Alaskans, and Chicanos.

We belong to AMCAS, the American Medical College Association Service. When the student wants to apply to medical school, for most medical schools in the United States, he or she applies to AMCAS in Washington, DC. The student is asked to fill out one form for all, and AMCAS then sends that form to all of the schools the student wishes to apply to.

The school then receives in the mail the AMCAS application, which has biographical data and information on activities in school and out, both college-related and outside of the university. It contains a personal essay in which they can write anything they want. The application also contains biographical information and detailed information on grade point averages broken down several ways—for the sciences, for non-sciences, and for all courses and by each year of undergraduate college, and there is an indication of scores on the standardized exams and a transcript of courses taken in college and the grades received. All schools to which you apply get a copy of this.

Most schools, but by no means all, then require a supplementary application, and we are one of these schools. Students start to apply for admission on June 15, which is the earliest they can. By the end of July, we will have received about 400 applications and by the end of the application process, which is December 15, we will receive 5,400 applications for 104 spaces. Private schools in general receive more applications per unit of space than public schools because many of the state schools are restrictive and must legally give preference to residents of the state.

In the supplementary applications that we send the students, we ask that they express themselves on a variety of subjects, which helps us to get to know the students better. They send this back with letters of recommendation from people with whom they have worked or studied.

The admissions committee consists of eight faculty members and four students, each of whom has been assigned to screen applications from a given geographical area. Each application is then assigned to the committee member for schools in that area, and he or she reviews the application and then decides if the person should be invited in for an interview, or if he or she should be rejected, or placed on hold for later review after seeing what the applicant pool for the year looks like.

If the faculty member's decision is to interview the student, the student is invited to come in for an interview at his or her convenience. Some schools will assign a date but are flexible and will reschedule if this is not convenient for the student, or they may tell the student to come in any given period, say between now and a few weeks later. It's a terribly expensive process for the student, and chances are the students that we interview are very good and will be invited to interview at other schools. By giving them options for scheduling interviews, this helps them to gang their interviews so that they can have several at schools in the same area at about the same time. Thus we may have fifteen kids come in for an interview on one day, and they may well have seen each other at Northwestern, Loyola, or whatever.

Usually they come in for three interviews: one with someone on the committee, usually with the person who suggested that they come in for an interview; then with a faculty member at large; and finally with a student. We give them an orientation to the school, which either I or the dean of students handles, and a talk by the financial aid officer, who discusses financing a medical education, and a senior medical student will talk to them about life at our school. They may then go to lunch with a freshman or sophomore medical student, students who are about the same age as the applicant, and they then tour the medical center. Altogether they will spend about a day on all phases of the interview and orientation. Most other schools do about the same. Some schools give one interview only, some two, and some three. At some schools, only the admissions committee does the interviewing, and at some this is handled by the faculty at large.

After the interview, the interviewer fills out his or her report, and faculty members write their comments. When all comments are back, the person who first recommended the interview then presents the application with all of the comments, and the committee votes to accept the application, reject it, or hold it for future decision.

All good schools oversubscribe—they overbook. The accepted students are extremely good and have probably been accepted to more than one school— this is true of about 85 percent of the students that we accept. Most good students will apply to twelve to fifteen or more schools, and the very good students will most likely receive several offers of admission. Thus we know that we will lose a certain number of students that we have accepted, so we overbook, and all of the other schools do the same.

By mid-May we tell the students to please make up their minds and that we must know their decision. In deciding, the applicants consider curriculum, exposure to patients, research opportunities, financial aid packages received from the various schools, and whether their prospective spouse will be accepted into law school there, whether they want to be close to parents or away from them, and other such factors. As they decide you hope that the number of acceptances falls below the class size, but not far below, by only about one or two spots, say. You would prefer not to have to go to the alternate pool at all, but to have the number of acceptances match the number of spaces. And at the same time, you don't want to oversubscribe and have too many acceptances.

What do we look for in a student? We look at the whole application. We have certain averages to be sure, but are more concerned with the overall student. True, the average acceptable grade point is 3.65, and for MCAT, it is about 11. But we accept some students whose grade point is below average, but falls somewhere in the range of 3.0 to 4.0 and an MCAT which is below 11, or part above average and part below average.

So, for example, if a student has a 3.3 grade point average, below our average norm for medical school admission, it may work out as follows:

2.5 for the freshman year

3.0 as a sophomore

3.5 as a junior and

4.0 as a senior

That's a positive indication of a kid who has pulled up his grades and is doing very well, or they may have had an off year, due to a death in the family or some personal problems—illness or whatever. We try to make sense of their record. They do not need an excuse, but an explanation as to why they fell down.

This is also true of their MCAT scores—there may be some very good reason why they did not do well on some part of the MCAT. This is especially true of recent immigrant students who usually have very low reading scores. They are not necessarily poor readers, but read more slowly. They may have super grades in every other area of the test, but average only 4 in the reading instead of the average of 8 for other students. We're willing to allow and accept that.

Then we look at the letters of recommendation that come from the professors and see what they say. They may say that this kid has grades that are not terribly impressive but that he or she is working twenty hours a week and is volunteering at the hospital throughout schooling and doing tutoring as well. These letters of recommendation are very important in helping us to understand the interpretation of students' course grades and test scores.

Sometimes we get applications from students with a 4.0 grade point average and incredible scores in standardized tests, but that's all they do. They may have enormous talent, but are one dimensional. They are not using their talent wisely. So we're looking for a more well-rounded student, one who wants to play in the symphony orchestra or to play sports or who does volunteer activities or is involved in campus politics. It could be any worthwhile activity, as long as they expend some of their efforts outside of themselves in behalf of others.

We then decide if the student is academically qualified and suitable for our school, in other words, a good fit. If the kid is from a rural background, for instance, and wants to practice family medicine in Montana, this is not the best school for him. We produce the highest percentage of any medical school in the country—nearly 25 percent of every graduating class—who go full time into academics. So we have to consider who we are, what the student's undergraduate record and grade point average are, and we put certain students in jeopardy by admitting them here, no matter how great they are.

So we bring them in for an interview and further try to determine their suitability from these personal talks. That is why we have somebody on the committee who has seen their record interview them and also a faculty member who has not seen their record. We want to see what they are like as people and if they would fit in here and get an idea of their aptitude at self-expression, the depth of their thought processes as they handle ambiguous situations, their social skills, all kinds of things. I don't think there is any medical school in the country that would give up the interview. It's a valuable tool.

As to minority students, those of various ethnic and racial groups that are underrepresented in medical school, including African-Americans, native Americans, Puerto Ricans, and Chicanos—the number of qualified minority applicants with the academic skills to go to U.S. medical schools has not increased in ten years—it has been absolutely flat. We get about 400 applicants a year from minority student ranks. The number has not changed in a long time. The receptivity of medical schools is very high. If you are a minority student and are qualified for U.S. medical school, you are heavily recruited. Schools fall all over themselves to make it attractive for minority students to matriculate there. We're not about to solve the problem of providing for the ethnic and racial diversity of physicians because we may increase the number of minority students in our medical school from five to ten, but that's at the expense of some other school. It does not solve the problem.

All of the medical schools twenty years or so ago gave preference to the typical applicants—kids out of undergraduate school, age twenty or twenty-one, in three-piece suits, preferably with an Ivy League background. Now the average age of matriculating students every year at medical schools across the country has gone up and up. There are several very good reasons for this. For one, students are taking a year or two years between college and medical school to grow a little, so they are more mature and experienced when they apply, and that's good, and, secondly, medical schools are much more receptive to people who have been in another profession and who may want to enter medical school or who go from business to medicine. The oldest applicant this year was forty-seven, and we took him. And this is a national trend.

The number of women in medical school in the last twenty years has gone from about 8 percent of the total class to a little more than 40 percent. Formerly we took younger students because it was a tradition.

There is no strong sentiment to increase or decrease the number of medical students. About 16,000 medical students enter medical school each year. You hear people saying that there are too few physicians or too many. There is a maldistribution of students, which is not necessarily a problem related to the number of students we are training. I don't think we understand which way to go nationwide as to the number of students trained in medical school.

We find that students tend to want to go away from home for undergraduate college. They want to break the ties with home and then return here for professional school, and 40 percent of all medical students wind up practicing in their home state. Harvard, for instance, would have about 40 percent of their students come from New England in general. At Stanford about 40 percent of their students are from California. While we do accept students for merit, we do get a higher percentage of students applying from Illinois. We tell students on their visit here to consider very hard why they want to go to medical school and what they expect of it. There are all sorts of subtle messages in the society in which we live about the desirability of being a doctor. Some people are receptive to these messages, but should be asking themselves what needs do they expect to fill by becoming a doctor. They may not have thought much about this. But they must understand as best as they can their motivation and then be able to explain this to a peer or to one of their teachers, because they are sure going to have to convince me that this is a wise decision. So I try to help them with these little tricks when I ask them, "What other careers have you considered that might appeal to you?" "Why do they appeal to you?" As a prospective student, you must make a decision that you can be happy with and understand because you are going to wind up in a very intense environment over a period of time in which the motivation must come from you. So the assumption is that when you walk through that door you know why you are there and want to provide your own motivation and persevere even when things are overwhelming. Coping with being an adult is being able to sort it all out.

I also ask applicants to make a list of the most important influences on their decision to enter medical school—parents, teachers, environment, the media, whatever—and then try to assess those influences. Are they good ones or not? Are you being pushed into this by your parents? Is this their decision or yours? Pleasing your parents is one of the worst reasons for trying to go to medical school.

Fortunately, our attrition rate is low—only about 1 percent—and this is true nationwide. Attrition often involves kids who are pushed into medicine. They get here, clear the hurdle of entry into school, and they die. It's really sad to see.

DEAN OF STUDENTS AND CHIEF FINANCIAL OFFICER

The thing that I usually tell students is that financing their education is as important as finding out about the curriculum of the medical school. As they begin the process, they should write and ask for a financial aid pamphlet. This will help them to get the information they need to get their questions on finances answered if they are invited to that school for an interview.

Obviously the schools are divided between public and private and depending upon the state in which the student lives—for instance, here in Illinois we only have in the city of Chicago six medical schools—one public and the rest, private. So if you say your home school or home state will provide you advantages, that may or may not be true but generally speaking, public schools are going to cost less to attend.

Also there is a movement afoot because the competition for places in medical school is so strong right now, there are three applicants for every place. And so what the students are doing is casting a broader net to seek out enough applications in hopes of being considered. So, if a student applies to a state institution, but it's not in their home state, the cost of education in that institution is almost as much as private school.

So there are really three groups of schools to apply to: the truly public—if you are an Illinois student, you apply to the University of Illinois and you pay the lower tuition as an Illinois resident, substantially less than you would pay at a private school. And if you are not an Illinois resident, you would pay out of state tuition, which is more expensive than some of the private institutions. And what I encourage students to do is to try to gather information about the availability of resources that the institution has for its students.

And in fact the student sometimes will find that given the financial aid packages available at private institutions, it costs them only a small amount more to attend a private school than a public school. So looking at the school's resources now becomes critical.

What we try to do is to give out average debt figures so that the students have some sort of ballpark figures as they are looking at schools and available sources of aid. The graduating class of 1994 is the only one in which we have aggregate data right now. In the public institution the average indebtedness is $55,000 and for private institutions it is about $79,000. And the average for public and private school indebtedness was around $65,000 per student.

But the important thing here is that a $65,000 debt is not a $65,000 debt because in the repayment years, this will be dictated by the kind of loan they had in medical school. That's what they really need to know.

Watch out if you go to an institution and they say to you: "Our student budget for this year is $46,000 and we have very limited resources to offer students—we have no loans available and we have no scholarships available and we have none whatever of our own." But they do have access to all of these private unsubsidized loan programs that are much more costly.

You've got what we call "good money" and then there's "bad money." And the way I try to describe this to students is to try to give them a sense of the different types of money that are available to pay for a medical education.

Many students have borrowed the Perkins loan—from the Perkins Federal Loan program. That has a 5 percent interest rate where they do go into repayment during the residency program, which they never used to. But for every dollar that the student borrows on the Perkins loan program, the student pays back $1.27 cents, so that's quite good money in terms of repayment.

Then there's the Federal Stafford program, which has been very well used over the years. It's now moved to a variable interest rate and it fluctuates with the T-bills. Right now, it's relatively low, in terms of overall interest. I think it's running $5^3/_4$ or somewhere in that area, so it's really quite good as well. If they borrow that money for every dollar that they get, they will repay about $1.51. So the thing we want students to understand is this: first, they should understand that money loaned must be repaid, that loans are subsidized with taxpayer dollars and so they are not paying interest while they are in school. Someone else is picking up that cost.

But that on the less good money, they're paying interest while they are in school, but what happens here is that the principal expands as you repay the loan, and this makes the cost of these loan dollars very, very expensive.

There are all kinds of private outfits out there that would like to loan to medical students—much as MedAccess, Med Achiever, and Med Assist—everybody's got a program for the medical student. On paper they'll loan the student on the same kind of arrangement as some of the good loans, but what you need to know is that for every dollar you borrow from these programs, you're likely to repay $3.00.

And that's why when you say—$50,000 debt—that doesn't sound too bad. But $50,000 of one of these loans where you're paying three times the amount for every dollar loaned is a lot different than $50,000 where you are only paying $1.27 for every dollar. So, understanding what the school can do is critical.

We also tell students that there are really three methods of financing a medical education. One is the family and student's own resources. Some students in this category never come to a financial aid office. They don't need it. There's about 20 percent of all medical students for whom this is a possibility.

But the larger percentage obviously are either borrowing against future income, which is the largest group, or they're spending their time in service for the money they borrow.

The military has been a mainstay for the service commitment kind of medical program. They don't require that the student commit to any particular specialty. But the students are required to pay their military debt off first and usually that's a year's service for every year that they participate in the program.

They have programs where you can participate in the second or third year or the fourth year, but if you take it for one year, that's the minimum.

But it should be noted that there are limitations on the number of positions they can offer. And the student should understand that if they want to go to school where and when they want to, they probably should not do the military. They must understand what it is that they are committing themselves to in accepting a military scholarship. And if they say they would rather not leave an institution with $100,000 in debt, I am going to commit my three or four years as a generalist, pay for my time off as a general medical officer through military service, and then get into a residency program and subspecialize and do what I want and I won't have $100,000-plus debt hanging over me. That's the choice the student makes. And if they can't do those things, then you've got to look at something else.

Now the second way of paying for your schooling in service is through the National Health Service Corps. And this agency, like many federal health agencies, has also been under fire. And there are real questions about, "Is it better to accept funding for medical school that you know you will have to pay back, or is it better in the military, where for every year committed, you are going to give them back a year of service?" The National Health Service Corps is restrictive in that you must be willing to commit to primary care. This is often problematic for some of the students when they come in because they don't know if primary care is what they want to do. It seems like now it's a recognized national need where there's a lot of pressure on the student to go into primary care.

But their definition of primary care is a little broader than others. For instance, they will include OB, general and family practice, internal medicine, but they also include geriatrics and perhaps psychiatry and a few other things. Now there are at least thirty-four organizations at the state level. For instance, here the Illinois Department of Public Health administers a program that is modeled after the National Health Service program. And again students that want to be in the national health service, but want to be in their own state and provide service in their own state, should look into these opportunities as well.

But the question that the government is struggling with now with regard to the National Health Service Corps is if they want to put more funding in the physician repayment side because that way they are not funding an education for students who may or may not commit to what it is they need.

I have not recently seen figures on what they were paying but it was formerly in the area of $20,000-$22,000 a year for a minimum of two years. And if they stay a third or fourth year, students get paid at the rate of $30,000 a year for those two years. And so for four years of service a student can retire a substantial medical school debt, and they earn a stipend to cover their living expenses as well while they are in school.

And there are also several programs for surgeons that are offered through the National Institutes of Health if you are interested in academic medicine. And you work off your debt the same as the National Health Service program as a research scholar or at the NIH. And like the National Health Service program, you receive $22,000 a year for every year that you commit to. So those are very nice programs, but they are very restricted and there's a lot of competition for them. But as I recall there are 110 spots altogether for the primary care students.

Then there's the Health Professions Student Loan program—the HPSL—there was a major shift in that program in 1993 in that we will allow you to take a student who is currently enrolled in your school and keep them in a professional student loan program, and it was somewhat like the Perkins subsidized loan in that there was 5 percent interest and they could defer interest payments until they completed their residency. So that was the best money available, bar none. And a lot of that money is cycling around in medical schools—millions and millions of dollars. The program has been around for many years.

But one of the ways to accomplish the federal mandate to train more primary care physicians is they just turned the entire loan program over to primary care loans. Not only is this now limited to primary care loans, but it is very restricted to those who would go into general internal medicine, general pediatrics, family medicine, geriatrics, and preventive care. There is no psychiatry or anything else funded in this program. Now if a student comes into medical school and is interested in one of these primary care loans, the schools are supposed to have committees to determine if this is a reality for this student. Now if the student borrows through this program for four years here, this would total about $104,000 loan debt strictly from this program. And if they did a pediatrics residency in their third year and decided that they wanted to go into pediatric cardiology, they would be faced with somewhat severe penalties for wanting to make that change. What would happen to that individual would be this information would then go back to the institution and they would have to recalculate from the time the first loan was made—take that total loan and convert it into a 12 percent interest loan. This then would be compounded and they would make the student pay it back in three years. And I calculate that for our students that would come to approximately $35,000 a year for three years.

This is the penalty that the student would have to pay under this program, if they don't remain in their primary care program.

So what we do is this: We wait until the student completes their third year and at that time the schools are allowed to buy back some of the high cost loans and give it out as primary care money. And there are penalties if you don't spend your allotted money, or if you have excess cash on hand, and you have to return this to the federal government. And they in turn will distribute this money to programs that have need of it.

And the other category that is separate from this is for the students who are interested in research, and obviously the Medical Scientist Training Program is very attractive if they know ahead of time that they want to do research. These are highly competitive and highly sought after positions within medical school, and there are probably fewer than 175 positions in all in the country. And this offers full funding for seven or eight years. And that can turn out to be a very tidy amount of perhaps well over $200,000 for seven years. So this is very limited, but for the students who are focused on doing research, it's excellent.

Now about 66 percent of our students have to get loans from the school while they are here. So we also have our own internal loans at 5 percent interest and we have a fair amount of scholarships, so we have about $3.5 million a year in resources to offset a $10 million need. And while this is a modicum of dollars to put toward need, it still will not make up the funds that the students will need to meet their medical school costs. That's where the students can turn to subsidized federal programs such as the Stafford Loan Program, where they can borrow $8,500; the Perkins loan, which is at the discretion of the school; and their own internal loan money if it's subsidized. And that is your primary source of student funding for medical school.

Now the subsidized loans—the ones that used to be very big in the portfolio—are not available for new incoming borrowers. They are available to those who have had them in the past, but the program is being phased out.

So the combinations that we have used in the past are the subsidized Stafford for $8,500 per year and the unsubsidized for $10,000 a year, for each year, plus other money that the school may have such as the Perkins loan. Or they may shift to the alternative loan programs now and go into some of the unsubsidized sources to make the package.

Now one of the things that we ask of our seniors, after they finish school, concerning scholarships is, "Were you awarded a scholarship at any time during your four years from the Association of American Medical Colleges?" We found that 60 percent of our students said that yes, they had some sort of a scholarship as opposed to 39 percent who didn't.

So obviously it's important that you get all of this information on the programs and what they cost, what the options are, and if you want to give time in service for funds received or if you are interested in research. If you are borrowing money, which includes 60 to 70 percent of all medical students in the country, what you want to do is first take a look at that student budget. And we encourage the students to set their goals to live under that budget, and there are ways they can do that. For one, you could get three roommates and share an apartment, and you can't afford to go to $7.50 movies to see a show; go to campus film showings at a fraction of the cost. You have to limit your calls home.

What students have been doing to make their student budget stretch is to avoid credit card usage. Now there is not a school in the country that can allow students to live at the levels that they would like to live; so if they get into credit card problems, they should analyze costs. If they think that $3.00 repayment for a dollar loaned is bad, they should just calculate what credit borrowing will cost them.

And if they have problems with repayment, their credit worthiness will be challenged, and at this point now a lot of student loans cannot be obtained if the borrower is not creditworthy. So we encourage students to get rid of their credit card debt before they head for medical school, and tear up their credit cards, and then they need to figure out how they can live like a student while they're in medical school. If they live like a physician while they're in medical school, they will live like a student when they are a physician. So it's their choice and they need to know what they are doing.

Many of our students also work. Many students feel that working is out of the realm of possibility. But there are things they can do. For instance, they can work as teaching assistants, which can net a student anywhere from $1,800 to $2,400 a quarter. Now that can really help meet budget costs. You've got to work for that money, but that money is yours and it doesn't come with a promissory note. So we encourage students to figure out ways to cut their costs and what they can do to earn some extra income. And then basically there are tons of outside scholarships that are available. But you have to look for them. You've got to go to the library and check all of the books that are out there on where to get financial aid, and then figure out any and all loans or funds that they might qualify for, and they should apply for these. Last year we had twenty to twenty-five students who were able to write away for scholarships and for which they qualified, and this amounted to a total of about $110,000 in outside scholarships alone. So being assertive and asking is absolutely critical.

But even so we are seeing a lot of indebtedness, much of it in the $100,000 or more category. Right now, this includes about 24 percent of our students. And within two to three years we figure that it will be 40 percent in this category.

So the likelihood of borrowing $100,000 for a medical school education is very much a reality today for anyone who wants to attend a private institution.

So what you have to do is to begin to keep an eye on the marketplace, because there are lots of changes in this marketplace for physicians. There is a physician oversupply. They have to say to themselves, "Well, gee, I've always wanted to be a neurosurgeon, but the number of neurosurgeons is in tremendous oversupply." And physicians' incomes have been going down, but they are still very good in comparison with a lot of other occupations. But there are some tradeoffs that the student should realize.

Indebtedness is going up to pay for medical school, and the prospects of earning high incomes in certain areas of medicine are going down. So the student needs to be very wary of borrowing too much, and they need to learn to do some sacrificing, which is not easy.

Now through Free Application for Federal Student Assistance, called the FAFSA, and because medical students are independent students, they can fill out their own personal information about what their earnings are, what their assets are, and this then is transmitted to the various places that do a needs analysis. That information is then transmitted to the schools, and the schools then can use that as the basis for awarding federal loan programs.

And we tell students that if they only want to borrow the $8,500 of subsidized Stafford and the $10,000 of unsubsidized Stafford, then they can borrow some money from the Perkins fund, if that's available. And this can all be done as an independent student and not having to turn in other sources of information.

So that in a nutshell is the package for determining financial aid. You go to the school's financial aid office, they go through your own budget and make a determination of how much the student can contribute, and they look at need and what the school can provide through the various loan and scholarship funds to meet these needs, and that's what the student has to know.

Then we can determine what the student is expected to contribute, what the parents are asked to contribute, and what the school can do in the way of loans and scholarship to meet their anticipated school needs. Sometimes, if the parents are unable to provide the money that we say they should, we will refer the students to these more expensive alternative loan funds if the student is unable or unwilling to work to make up the difference.

So in sum, there's all sorts of money out there to pay for a medical education, but the problem is to get the best dollars you can so that the total indebtedness is not more than you can handle years after you graduate.

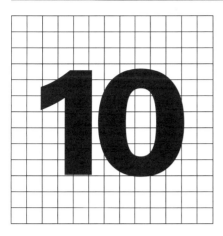

THE SPECIALTIES AND SUBSPECIALTIES

This chapter lists the medical specialty areas and the major subspecialties that have been accredited as of September 1994. New specialties are constantly being developed and certified, but as of late 1994, these were the major divisions of medicine, as recognized by the American Board of Medical Specialties and other organizations involved in the training and certification of medical specialists. For more information about training requirements of the various specialties listed, write to the certifying board or specialty society for that particular specialty at the addresses given in Appendix B.

ALLERGY AND IMMUNOLOGY

Originally a subspecialty of pediatrics and internal medicine, allergy and immunology received specialty status with the formation of the American Board of Allergy and Immunology in 1972.

Allergists and immunologists are involved with the strange overreaction of the body's immune system to external stimulants or allergens. Ordinarily such stimulants trigger desirable reactions to head off such invaders as pollen or dirt before they can enter the body, but sometimes such reactions can result in discomfort and pain, even danger. Take, for instance, a person who is allergic to penicillin. To most people, penicillin is a safe and highly effective way to combat various infections, but to the person who is allergic to penicillin, this agent can produce real problems—from welts on the hands and the feet to a very dangerous reaction known as anaphylaxis, which stems from an overproduction of antibodies to penicillin or other allergens.

Ordinarily, however, most people suffering from allergy are treated for milder forms of the disease—such as sniffles, sneezing, itchiness, and skin reactions, including eczema and welts.

To treat the symptoms of allergy, the allergist tests the patient with a series of small doses of various substances, including a wide variety of foods and other allergens ranging from cat and dog dander to pollen, dust, and ragweed. If the patient registers positive, the doctor administers a series of injections consisting of small doses of the substances to which the patient is allergic. Thus the patient builds up a gradual immunity to the substances in the same way that a patient who is immunized to polio, smallpox, or diphtheria builds up an immunity to those diseases.

Since treatment can last for years, the allergist's practice consists of treating all old patients plus whatever new ones come in. Specialists in the field are predominantly involved in clinical medicine, although some go into academic research. Because treatments are often lengthy and last years, allergists often form close relationships with their patients. And since, as is often the case, members of the same family may share the same allergies, the doctor may treat several members of the same family in much the same manner as does the family practitioner.

Hours are fairly regular since most patients are healthy in other respects, although the wheezing associated with one form of allergic reaction, asthma, can be dangerous and can occur at any time, day or night.

In addition to the conditions listed above, allergists often treat patients for food and drug reactions and AIDS.

In 1994 there were 85 officially accredited training programs in allergy and immunology and 15 programs in an accredited subspecialty—clinical and laboratory immunology. Three years of residency in either internal medicine or pediatrics is required, followed by a two-year fellowship in allergy and immunology. For further information contact the American Academy of Allergy and Immunology.

ANESTHESIOLOGY

Primarily anesthesiologists work behind the scenes in hospital operating and emergency rooms administering anesthetics (drugs) to patients undergoing surgery, dental procedures, and to mothers to be in the delivery of their babies. The object, of course, is to make the procedures as pain free as possible. In most cases the patient is completely under, or oblivious to pain. In monitoring the delivery of anesthetics to patients involved in various operations, the anesthesiologist is called on to render life and death decisions involving the patient's vital signs—pulse, blood pressure, and respiration—at a complicated console used to control the input of anesthetic and to monitor its effects on the patient.

To support their work, anesthesiologists must have a vast background in physiology and pharmacology. Their hours can be long if they are the only physician on duty at a small but busy hospital, although ordinarily their hours are fairly predictable, except for emergencies that can arise at any time.

Ordinarily, patient contact is limited to pre- and postsurgery visits, at which the anesthesiologist may describe the procedure and thus help to relieve patient anxiety. The anesthesiologist must be able to react coolly and swiftly under stress and may be called on to adroitly manipulate a bag containing anesthetic or pure oxygen. Surgery procedures handled by the anesthesiologist range from simple tonsillectomies to complex open-heart surgery. Training involves a base year, or internship, followed by three years of training in clinical anesthesiology and critical care. Approximately 149 programs are offered per year in anesthesiology, as well as 46 in critical care management and 55 in pain management.

A few programs offer training in special areas of anesthesiology—pediatrics, obstetrics, and neurosurgery, for instance—that often can be applied for separately from regular anesthesiology training programs.

Unpredictable hours and the need to occasionally work overtime make this a stressful but high paying field at times. In 1994 anesthesiologists averaged approximately $231,000 per year. Predictions are for an oversupply of practitioners in this field by 1996. Sponsoring organizations are the American Board of Anesthesiology, AMA Council on Medical Education, and American Society of Anesthesiologists.

CARDIOLOGY

Also referred to as cardiovascular disease, cardiology is a leading subspecialty of internal medicine. Cardiology deals primarily with diseases of the heart and the circulatory system. Although in the past the field was primarily concerned with analysis of the patient's symptoms for diagnosis, today many practitioners devote a considerable part of their practice to performing various diagnostic tests themselves, such an angiography, an invasive procedure to determine the location and amount of blockage in a patient's coronary arteries. Regardless of the tests involved, whether it be a regular EKG or a Holter monitor (a device that provides a continuous EKG over a twenty-four hour period) or a stress test, which studies the patient's EKG under stress (as seen on a treadmill), the cardiologist is called on to provide expert analysis of the tests and arrive at a diagnosis and plan for treatment.

The field is very fast moving, and new developments are being reported almost every week. Cardiology presents a challenge for doctors who wish to be on the cutting edge of technology and for those who like working with and supporting patients. At the same time, however, heart patients are often quite ill and the work can be physically and emotionally draining. The financial rewards are considerably greater than those of the internist.

Training in the approximately 209 residency programs involves completion of a two- to three-year fellowship in cardiology following completion of a three-year residency in internal medicine.

COLON AND RECTAL SURGERY

Formerly known as proctology, the name of this surgical specialty was changed to reflect the broader scope of the field. Specialists in this branch of medicine treat and diagnose disorders of the intestinal tract, the rectum, and anal as well as perianal areas.

Although they are surgeons, these physicians offer a variety of diagnostic and medical treatments, including endoscopy and colonoscopy. Diseases commonly treated include hemorrhoids, polyps, cancer, fissures, colitis, and diverticulitis. Most patients seen are referred by primary care physicians, hence practitioners in this field are located primarily in midsize to large cities.

Specialists tend to spend a good deal of time in their offices and in the hospital, and since emergencies are rarely encountered, the hours on the job are more regular than those of most physicians. Most conditions are relatively easy to diagnose and treat, which is one of the primary reasons students choose this particular specialty.

The training is among the lengthiest of all medical specialties involving a five-year residency in general surgery followed by a fellowship of one or two years in colon and rectal surgery. Average gross yearly income for all surgical specialties, including colon and rectal surgery, was $275,000 in 1994—higher than for general surgery, which was $222,000 a year.

As one of the smaller surgical specialties, (there were 29 residency programs in 1994), there are more applicants for training than there are programs. The closest field to colon and rectal surgery in osteopathy is proctology, which is more limited in scope.

Sponsoring organizations are the American Board of Colon and Rectal Surgery, AMA Council on Medical Education, and American College of Surgeons.

DERMATOLOGY

The focus of the dermatologist is vast consisting as it does of the skin, the cover that encases the entire body. Besides furnishing the heart, brain, and other vital organs a protective covering, the skin houses many sensory nerves and serves as an early warning for such hazards as extreme heat or cold and other potentially dangerous agents.

Besides understanding the physical manifestations of disease that can affect the skin, the dermatologist must be able to cope with and understand the emotional aspects that often accompany such problems as eczema and acne. The latter is a particularly sensitive area for teenagers. Fortunately, since most skin conditions are easily observed, most patients come to the dermatologist in the early stages when the conditions are most easily treated.

Night calls are seldom encountered, aside from hospital follow-up after surgery and cases of severe itching or severe burn. Such surgery is usually handled by the dermatologist in the office, usually by cautery.

One of the most serious problems treated by the dermatologist is skin cancer, which is often noticed by the patient or his or her family or friends in its earlier stages. Usually, except for a more serious form of cancer known as melanoma, skin cancers are easily removed by surgery and cauterizing. They involve close follow-up to make sure there are no recurrences. Melanoma is a condition requiring very early and quick treatment by the dermatologist.

In cases of severe allergic reactions, the dermatologist may be assigned to cover the manifestations of the disease that cause itchiness or scaly skin. Besides removal of skin tumors and cancer, the dermatologist deals with such conditions as warts, acne, and eczema.

To qualify for this specialty, you must complete a four-year residency, including three years in dermatology. Dermatopathology and dermatological immunology, two subspecialties of dermatology, require additional training. There are approximately 103 programs in dermatology and 39 in dermatopathology.

EMERGENCY MEDICINE

Emergency medicine specialists, who practice primarily in hospital emergency rooms, are trained to respond to, diagnose, and treat a wide array of conditions and emergencies that present themselves. Conditions range from removal of a marble lodged in the throat of a small child to treating gunshot wounds and stabbing victims and victims of car accidents who may have multiple fractures and massive internal bleeding.

Physicians in this specialty are trained to stabilize patients with a vast array of life-threatening conditions, and they must be able to act coolly and swiftly under such circumstances. Since emergency victims arrive at any hour, day or night, and cases can involve various medical and surgical procedures to stabilize the patient, hours can be quite lengthy. Seldom, however, do emergency physicians receive calls outside of assigned working hours. Since the work is twenty-four hours a day, these specialists may be called on often to work schedules that involve late nights and weekends, and that can change from day to day. This could be quite stressful.

Due to the nature of the work, where emergency physicians seldom have any control as to who their patients may be, rarely are they able to form lasting relationships with patients. They must be prepared to care for and treat anyone who comes through the door at any time.

Most of the 102 training programs require three or more years of training in emergency medicine following completion of an internship in internal medicine, surgery, or family practice.

Emergency physicians certified in medical toxicology have special additional knowledge in the treatment of patients exposed to poisoning through the use of drugs and household or industrial toxins.

The pediatric emergency physician has special qualifications to manage and treat emergencies in infants and small children.

Finally, to be certified in sports medicine, the emergency physician specializing in this area is responsible for the care of those involved in sports, not only for treatment of emergencies that may arise, but in the prevention of injury and illness as well.

ENDOCRINOLOGY, DIABETES, AND METABOLISM

Endocrinologists, who are subspecialists in internal medicine, limit their practices to diseases of the body's endocrine, or glandular, systems. This includes diseases associated with the thyroid and pituitary glands, and hormonal secretions associated with various other glands. But probably accounting for the majority of patients seen are those with diabetes, a disease involved with disorders of the pancreas in which the system produces too much sugar.

Endocrinologists are often involved in problems connected with nutrition and metabolism or absorption of food, and with hypertension. Like cardiologists, endocrinologists are primarily involved with analyzing patient problems, evaluating patient symptoms, performing any necessary tests, and relying on his or her own physical examination to work out the diagnosis and treatment plan.

Primarily office based, these specialists rely on referrals for most patients. Training, which involves completion of a two- to three-year fellowship after completing a three-year residency in internal medicine, is offered in 141 programs.

FAMILY PRACTICE

Perhaps the prototype of the family practitioner was the general physician, who practiced in the days prior to the onset of specialization, roughly prior to 1940. At the time such physicians included the vast majority of doctors then practicing, and as family doctors they treated a wide array of ills and disorders affecting the entire family. These ranged from measles and whooping cough to surgery for cysts and warts, minor cuts, abrasions and fractures, and a host of other diseases and disorders, as well as the delivery of babies. Family practitioners, as they are now known, became a certified branch of medicine in 1969. Because of the wide range of diseases and complaints they see, family physicians must have a vast fund of medical knowledge, including medical diagnostic, testing, and treatment techniques, as well as knowledge of drugs and how they are used most effectively.

With the vast proliferation of medical knowledge and therapeutics in recent decades, they cannot be expert in all medical problems, but it is estimated that they can treat as many as 90 percent of the cases that are presented.

As is true of other primary care physicians—internists, pediatricians, and obstetrician-gynecologists—they are gatekeepers and sources of referral to other medical specialists when such expertise is called for.

In the past family physicians were solo practitioners working primarily out of their own offices, but this is no longer true with an estimated 40 percent of these doctors involved in group practices of one sort or another, while another 57 percent participate in various alternative health plans (HMOs, PPOs, and IPAs).

The work calls for infinite patience, tact, and understanding and an abundance of enthusiasm and sympathy in handling the entire array of medical problems that present themselves—from tiny infants to those in the geriatric category.

Although trained to deliver babies, this is not often a part of family practice today, primarily because of the difficulty and expense in obtaining liability (malpractice) insurance to cover this part of the practice.

The average family practitioner now devotes 56.5 hours per week to patient care, with approximately 60 percent of that time spent in office visits, 13 percent in hospital rounds, 14 percent in other patient visits, and 4 percent to surgery. At the same time, the income for family physicians is about the lowest of all physicians, averaging a gross income of about $116,800, which explains, at least in part, the difficulty of attracting students to this field in the past.

Even so, despite the long hours and the low salaries, family physicians often derive great satisfaction from following patients over many years, and they establish many close relationships with their patients.

Training available in 430 residency programs involves a year of internship and two years of residency. Sponsoring organizations are the American Board of Family Practice, AMA Council on Medical Education, and American Academy of Family Physicians.

With additional training a family physician can become certified for geriatrics, which means simply that such a specialist is trained to advise and treat the elderly in the prevention, diagnosis, and treatment of disorders common to them.

Similar to emergency medicine, specialists in family practice, with additional training, can become certified in sports medicine, thus specializing in the promotion of wellness and in the prevention of disease.

GASTROENTEROLOGY

Another very important subspecialty of internal medicine involving patients suffering from problems of the liver, pancreas, stomach, intestine, bowels, and gallbladder is gastroenterology, which is often referred to in the profession as GI (as in gastro*intestinal*) problems.

These specialists are primarily office based and rely on primary care physicians for referrals. They see a good mix of age groups and backgrounds. With the recent advances in technology, they have become increasingly involved with such procedures as using a lighted endoscope to visualize specific parts of the patient's digestive system. But primarily gastroenterologists rely on their own experience and skills in analyzing patient problems and use case histories for diagnosis and treatment.

One of the more lucrative subspecialties of internal medicine, gastroenterology can mean long hours. Training involves completion of a two- to three-year fellowship in gastroenterology preceded by a three-year residency in internal medicine. There are approximately 176 training programs in this field.

GENERAL SURGERY

Surgery is that vast branch of medicine that is concerned with the use of surgical techniques in treating patients with medical problems. The field is so broad that is has spawned a whole array of subspecialties, many of which have become specialties in their own right—thoracic surgery, urology, ophthalmology, and plastic surgery to name a few. Surgeons treat a variety of medical problems, including cancers of the digestive system, breast cancer, hernia, gallbladder removal, and cysts. The patients they treat represent all ages, though for the most part they are adults, because many children are treated by pediatric surgeons.

Surgeons are primarily results oriented; they derive great satisfaction out of being able to see the immediate results of their efforts. The uncertain and gray areas of medicine—where conditions are chronic and may resist efforts at a cure—are not for them. Most conditions they are called on to treat are one-time efforts, barring a recurrence, thus making long-term relationships with patients almost impossible. For the most part the surgeon's only patient contact may be just prior to and immediately after the surgical procedure.

The work calls for a cool head in an emergency, manual dexterity, and stamina—surgeons are often on their feet for hours at a time. Because they are sometimes called on to handle emergencies that can occur at any time, the surgeon has to anticipate calls that may upset normal family relationships. The hours are long, but the salary is excellent, exceeded only by those of various surgical subspecialties—cardiovascular, plastic, and urology, for example. The latter are more lucrative and no more demanding, although they do involve a lengthier training period.

On the whole the field is overcrowded, and current estimates call for a considerable surplus of practitioners in the immediate future. Residency training, available in some 330 programs, involves a year of internship and four years of general surgery. Additional subspecialty fellowships involving still more training are available in general, hand, and pediatric surgery; general vascular surgery; and surgical critical care.

Sponsoring organizations are the American Board of Surgery, American College of Surgeons, and AMA Council on Medical Education.

GERIATRICS

A growing subspecialty of internal medicine that reflects the rise in longevity of people today, geriatrics is associated primarily with treating disorders of the elderly.

Specialists in geriatrics bring to bear specific skills and understanding of the diseases affecting the elderly—arthritis, heart disease, diabetes, and high blood pressure, among others. Because many older patients have multiple medical problems and, therefore, may be taking several medications, these specialists must have a good understanding of how drugs interact, with specific relevance to the elderly.

Although a few thousand doctors are certified in this specialty, only a few hundred have had specific postgraduate training in this field. Most specialists complete residencies in either family practice or internal medicine and go on to take two to three years of additional training in roughly 85 programs to become certified as a specialist in geriatrics. As basically an internist who limits his or her practice to the elderly, this specialist's salary is roughly that of the internist. Patients are obtained primarily by word-of-mouth from one patient to another, or through other physicians.

Sponsoring organizations include the American Board of Internal Medicine, American Board of Family Practice, and AMA Council of Medical Education.

HEMATOLOGY

Specialists in the diseases of the bloodstream, including the blood, spleen, and lymph glands, are known as hematologists, and they constitute yet another subspecialty of internal medicine. Hematologists treat all organ systems, but always with reference to the blood chemistry and physiology of those systems. Among the blood disorders that they are called on to treat are leukemia, hemophilia, sickle cell anemia, lymphoma, and serious anemia. Although the practice is primarily office based, hematologists treat a good many inpatients on a consulting basis or as the primary physician. Night calls are often encountered, as are emergencies.

Training in hematology, usually a two-year fellowship, follows completion of three-year residencies in either pediatrics or internal medicine.

There are about 74 training programs in the field, which it is estimated will witness a shortage of practitioners in the near future.

Sponsoring organizations include the American Board of Internal Medicine, American Board of Pediatrics, and AMA Council on Medical Education.

INFECTIOUS DISEASES

As the name implies, specialists in this subspecialty of internal medicine are concerned primarily with infectious, or contagious, disease, affecting either young or old. As such the practice is extremely varied and ranges from everything from AIDS to pneumonia and tuberculosis.

Believed at one time to be largely obsolete as a result of antibiotics, these specialists are now surging in numbers because of the onset of AIDS and drug-resistant germs.

These doctors serve primarily as consultants to other physicians in cases that cannot be traced to any one disease, as, for instance, a patient running a high temperature with no obvious cause. In recent years these specialists are being called on to treat increasing numbers of AIDS patients.

Training, available in approximately 141 medical programs, consists usually of a two- to three-year fellowship following completion of a three-year residency in internal medicine.

Sponsoring organizations are the American Board of Internal Medicine and AMA Council on Medical Education.

INTERNAL MEDICINE

Often referred to as internists, these specialists are the largest group of all physicians, currently numbering about 95,000 practitioners.

Internal medicine is the spawning ground for many medical specialties, and a number of subspecialists—cardiologists, gastroenterologists, hematologists, and others—must first complete their training in internal medicine before qualifying for their subspecialty.

Generally speaking, the internist treats and diagnoses a variety of acute and chronic disorders affecting the organs and various internal body systems. In one day the internist may see patients suffering from a wide range of disorders including diabetes, arthritis, flu and colds, heart problems, and infectious diseases.

Internists differ from family practitioners in that their practice is limited to adults, although this might include adolescents as well; also, they ordinarily do not deliver babies. You can see that the practice is for all intents and purposes as broad and varied as that of the family practitioner and calls for a scope and range of medical knowledge that is equally broad.

And like family physicians, internists are at the beck and call of their patients, a part of the work that often intrudes on their personal lives and family ties. Like those in family practice, internists often develop close and satisfying ties with their patients over a long period of years.

Basically, internal medicine is cognitive in that such specialists are almost always attempting to diagnose and treat the various ills affecting their patients. This involves the use of tests, the doctor's own observations and probing, the patient's medical history, and the particular ill or disorder involved.

Because of their emphasis on the cognitive, or diagnostic aspect of medicine, internists are on the low end of the pay scale, averaging $180,900 in 1993.

Training in this specialty is three years and involves a year of internship followed by two years of residency in approximately 415 allopathic programs nationwide and about 46 osteopathic programs.

Interestingly, the earnings of many subspecialists in internal medicine are often much higher than those of internists. In such specialties as cardiology and urology, doctors are likely to perform procedures such as angiography in the case of cardiologists and lithotripsy in the case of urologists. This also serves to boost them into a higher paying reimbursement bracket. Internists' jobs, which are primarily cognitive or diagnostic, pay less.

Currently the field is undergoing a shortage of applicants, although with the current emphasis on primary care physicians as well as the proposed Resource Based Relative Value Scale, internal medicine is one of the specialties that would benefit through higher pay scales, which in turn would make the specialty more attractive to students.

Physicians with internal medicine certification can with two to three years of additional training be certified in sports medicine and adolescent medicine.

Sponsoring organizations are the American Board of Internal Medicine, AMA Council of Medical Education, and American College of Physicians.

MEDICAL GENETICS

The newest of the board-certified specialties, medical genetics aims at diagnosing and treating medical problems of patients with genetically linked diseases.

Specialists in this area are qualified to identify various genetic diseases with the use of cytogenic, radiologic, and biochemical testing. Through data thus obtained, the medical geneticist can counsel or initiate treatment, or work out plans for the prevention of genetic disease. Areas in which these specialists become involved include disorders of metabolism (problems of absorbing and digesting food), hemoglobin, chromosome abnormalities, and neural tube defects.

Training involves two years of residency in internal medicine or pediatrics and two additional years of training in any of the specialties listed below:

Clinical biochemical genetics.   These specialists are qualified to perform and interpret biochemical tests to help diagnose and manage genetic disorders.

Clinical biochemical/molecular geneticists.   These specialists are certified in both clinical biochemical genetics and in clinical molecular genetics.

Clinical cytogeneticists.   Practitioners in this field provide cytogenic laboratory services to diagnose and interpret genetic problems.

Clinical geneticists.   These genetic specialists are competent to provide comprehensive services in diagnosing, managing, and counseling patients with genetic abnormalities.

Clinical molecular geneticists.   Here genetics specialists are certified to perform and interpret molecular tests involved in the diagnosis and management of patient genetic disorders.

Medical geneticists.   These physicians serve as consultants to medical and dental specialists in the diagnosis and treatment of genetic disorders.

For information on certification contact the American Board of Medical Genetics or the AMA Council on Medical Education.

MEDICAL ONCOLOGY

Cancer—in all of its forms and as it affects the body systems and organs—is the concern of the specialist known as the oncologist. Because of the multi-system nature of the field, the oncologist is often called in as a consultant to work on various bodily organs, including the kidney, colon, liver, and so forth. Because the treatment of cancer at present is so often unpredictable, the oncologist, more so than any other physician, often must deal with the death of his or her patients, which can be very stressful.

Due to the fact that they tend to treat chronic conditions over a period of years, oncologists often develop very close relationships with their patients, and as new treatments and drugs are being developed they are meeting ever-increasing success. The patient mix is very diverse and the range of problems encountered quite varied.

Training, which consists of a two-year fellowship upon completion of a three-year residency in internal medicine, is offered in 84 programs. Sponsoring organizations include the American Board of Internal Medicine and AMA Council on Medical Education.

NEPHROLOGY

Kidney disorders and diseases of the urinary tract are the specialization of the nephrologist, yet another subspecialist in the field of internal medicine.

Nephrologists treat a variety of kidney disorders, including patients requiring kidney dialysis or kidney transplants as well as those suffering from renal failure, high blood pressure, or diabetes. Because of the rather narrow focus of their specialty, nephrologists are often able to help patients with chronic kidney disorders lead fairly normal lives. But as is often true of other internal medicine subspecialties, nephrologists are frequently called on to treat patients who are critically ill. The practice requires individuals who are well versed in chemistry and physiology as they apply to medicine.

Training in approximately 142 medical programs usually involves a two-year fellowship upon completion of a three-year residency in internal medicine.

Sponsoring organizations are the American Board of Internal Medicine, American Society of Nephrology, and AMA Council on Medical Education.

NEUROLOGICAL SURGERY

This branch of medicine deals with neurosurgery or brain surgery. Due to the delicate nature of the work, this highly specialized skill can have a profound influence on the outcome of the patient's problems. Sometimes the outcome is good; often it is not and can result in death or disability. The work is extremely challenging since the brain controls our ability to think, remember, move various limbs, and so forth. Because of the high stakes involved, most neurologists regard the work as a calling and not merely a practice. In addition to manual dexterity, the work calls for the ability to remain cool in the face of disappointment. New developments in the field of transplantation of fetal tissue and the use of microsurgery techniques promise a rise in the demand for doctors skilled in this specialty.

Hours are long and neurosurgeons are subject to call at any time of the day or night because accidents or injuries that can seriously affect the nervous system can happen at any time.

Among the conditions seen and treated are brain and spinal cord cancers, lumbar and cervical disk disease, aneurysms, and head and spinal cord trauma. Besides being able to work effectively under pressure, the neurosurgeon must understand the relationship of the anatomy and physiology to medical health, especially the impact on the nervous system.

This is one of the most challenging and lucrative of the medical specialties, with neurosurgeons averaging more than $408,000 in 1994. But it is also one of the most vulnerable to malpractice suits, and premiums for insurance coverage are among the highest for all surgical specialties.

To qualify for this specialty, you must complete a one-year residency in general surgery followed by five years of residency in neurological surgery in one of the 99 training programs offered.

Sponsoring organizations include the American Board of Neurological Surgery, American College of Surgeons, and AMA Council on Medical Education.

NEUROLOGY

Specialists in this field are concerned with the diagnosis and treatment of various disorders that can impair the functioning of the brain, spinal cord, peripheral nerves, muscles, and nervous system, as well as the blood vessels involved in these areas. Often this specialist is a consultant to other physicians in diagnosing and treating neurological problems. Because there are close ties between neurology and psychiatry, board certification is offered by a combined board of psychiatry and neurology.

Certification involves completion of four years of residency training including a three-year residency in neurology after completing one year in internal medicine. If you are primarily interested in child neurology, you must complete a two-year residency in pediatrics, or one year in pediatrics and another in internal medicine, prior to entering a three-year child neurology residency program. Currently 122 programs are offered in neurology and an additional 75 in child neurology.

Sponsoring organizations include the American Board of Neurology and Psychiatry and AMA Council on Medical Education.

NUCLEAR MEDICINE

A relatively new medical specialty established in 1971, nuclear medicine is primarily concerned with the use of radioactive materials to help visualize areas of the body and organs being studied with nuclear medicine equipment. Highly technical in its thrust and orientation, this is primarily a support specialty that assists primary care and other physicians in arriving at diagnoses. Patient contact is limited to the time when patients are involved in various nuclear testing procedures, including PET (Positive Emission Tomography), SPECT (Single Proton Emission Computerized Tomography), MRI (Magnetic Resonance Imaging), and other highly technical procedures of imaging used primarily for diagnostic studies. Nuclear medicine supplements and assists radiology (X-rays).

Currently the Joint Commission on Accreditation of Healthcare Organizations requires that hospitals of more than 300 beds must provide nuclear medical services under the direction of a qualified specialist in nuclear medicine. Hence there are almost always positions to be found in this field in hospitals. As few practitioners can afford the cost of equipment, which is prohibitive, they are somewhat limited in their work by the nature and age of the equipment that they utilize.

The field is fast moving and changes in technology require constant study and schooling to keep abreast of what is happening.

These specialists are primarily concerned with solving or interpreting patient tests and have little patient contact outside of the imaging assignments that they perform.

Training involves a two-year residency in nuclear medicine after the completion of a two-year residency in either internal medicine, pathology, or radiology. About 190 positions are offered in 87 residency programs.

Sponsoring organizations include the American Board of Internal Medicine, American Board of Pathology, American Board of Radiology, and Society of Nuclear Medicine.

OBSTETRICS-GYNECOLOGY

Obstetrics-gynecology is a two-part speciality. The first part—obstetrics—deals with the care of women, before, during, and after giving birth. The second part—gynecology—treats diseases of the female reproductive system. Although some practitioners specialize in one part of the specialty or the other, most specialize in both and are qualified to do both.

Though the field offers great satisfaction in taking part in the birth process, it does have its negative side, primarily the high number of malpractice suits in the field.

Perhaps this is the result of the many medical advances in biomedical research. One of these advances, ultrasound, is a diagnostic technique that helps the doctor to follow the various stages of the fetus as it develops in the mother's womb from the early stages of pregnancy through full term. Not only can ultrasound establish the baby's true age, but a sample of amniotic fluid, which envelops the infant in the womb, can be checked to see if the child carries any genetic predisposition to such diseases as Down's syndrome, sickle-cell anemia, or Tay-Sachs disease.

Some experts theorize that as a result of profound medical advances such as ultrasound, patients may have exaggerated or unrealistic expectations of their obstetricians; others feel that competition from other specialists, primarily family physicians and nurse-midwives, has made the obstetrics part of the specialty less attractive to those who are concentrating on gynecology.

Other negative aspects of the work, particularly in obstetrics, are that practitioners are subject to call at any time of the day or night, and that means that the specialist must be prepared to run into a certain number of sleepless nights.

But most pregnant women are healthy, and it is doubtful if there is anything quite as satisfying in medicine as the birth of a normal and healthy child.

Under their gynecological cap, specialists in ob-gyne, as it is known in medicine, treat a variety of problems affecting the female reproductive system, including pelvic pain, endometriosis, yeast infections, and cancer of the reproductive organs.

Practitioners in this field therefore must be able to treat patients both medically and surgically as necessary and because of the hands-on nature of the work, they must have good manual dexterity.

Although the income is among the highest in all of medical practice, averaging $220,000 a year in 1994, this is somewhat counterbalanced by the unpleasant aspects of the work—such as long hours, being subject to calls at any time of the night or day, and the cost of malpractice insurance, among the highest of all medical specialties.

There are several areas of subspecialization within this field, including reproductive endocrinology, which deals primarily with problems of fertility; gynecological oncology, which involves cancer of the reproductive system; and maternal and fetal medicine, which deals primarily with high-risk pregnancies. All the subspecialties require additional training over and above the basic four-year residency program in ob-gyne.

Sponsoring organizations are the American Board of Obstetrics-Gynecology, American College of Obstetricians and Gynecologists, and AMA Council on Medical Education.

OPHTHALMOLOGY

Ophthalmology is the branch of medicine dealing primarily with diseases of the eye. Practitioners in this field do very delicate surgical work, while at the same time serve as primary care physicians to anyone with problems seeing or with eye care. Ophthalmologists rely on a wide range of complicated optical equipment in their work.

Although ophthalmologists spend much of their time in the office, there is a need for a special section of the hospital or clinic with trained staff and operating rooms, where they can handle other aspects of their work.

One of their most important duties is the prescription of eyeglasses, for which they rely on refraction equipment. This helps them determine the proper strength of lenses, which they then note in the form of a prescription for eyeglasses. But in the case of other more severe eye disorders, the ophthalmologist may have to turn to medical treatment or resort to surgery. Such conditions include glaucoma, a disease characterized by pressure in the eyeball, conjunctivitis, an inflammation of the eye membrane; other inflammatory eye problems; and finally, cataract.

It is this somewhat unique combination of medical and surgical treatment that makes the field so attractive and challenging. Because they deal with such a small and highly sensitive area of the body—the eye—and the physiological structures leading up to the eye, specialists in this area must have great eye-hand dexterity and technical skill.

Ophthalmologists see a mix of patients, young and old, many over long periods of time, and can thus form some very strong and long-lasting relationships with patients. But the training is long and rigorous, with most residencies running four years, including a year of internship.

This is a difficult field to enter, with an estimated surplus of 40 percent foreseen by Graduate Medical Education National Advisory Committee. Training is available through approximately 137 programs.

Hours are more predictable in this field since there are few life-threatening situations to contend with. The financial rewards are substantial, averaging gross incomes of $224,000 a year in 1994.

Sponsoring organizations include the American Board of Ophthalmology, and AMA Council on Medical Education.

ORTHOPEDIC SURGERY

Diseases of the musculoskeletal system, including the bones, muscles, joints, and connective tissue, are the area of concern of orthopedists, known more familiarly in the profession as orthopods. Their main concern is the maintenance of optimum functioning of the musculoskeletal system. Conditions that they see regularly in their practices are fractures; arthritis; degenerative diseases of the hip, knees, limbs, shoulders, and elbows; knee trauma; hip trauma and physical deformities.

Orthopods are often able to quickly relieve pain. Through surgery or a combination of surgery and other medical treatments such as physical therapy or massage, they are able to relieve many potentially crippling or disabling conditions, especially arthritis. Such happy outcomes make this a particularly attractive field, but the hours can be long, often twelve to fifteen hours a day.

This is one of the more difficult branches of surgery to enter as it involves a year or two in general surgery or other approved surgical or medical specialty followed by a residency of three years in orthopedic surgery.

Specialists in this field often like to work with their hands and have hobbies such as woodworking or carpentry, and many orthopods are sports minded. Indeed, sports medicine is a subspecialty of the field, as are a number of other programs including pediatric orthopedics, orthopedic oncology, hand surgery, and foot and ankle surgery, all of which require training over and above that needed or orthopedic surgery.

Earnings are high with specialists reportedly averaging $288,000 a year, but this is counterbalanced somewhat by the cost of malpractice insurance, which is very high, as is the cost of equipment and office overhead.

Sponsoring organizations are the American Board of Orthopaedic Surgery, American Academy of Orthopaedic Surgery, and AMA Council on Medical Education.

OTOLARYNGOLOGY

This specialty deals with the head, ear, nose, and throat—often referred to as ENT (ear-nose-throat) in the profession. It covers practically all ills in these areas except those requiring the attention of ophthalmologists (for the eyes) and brain surgeons and neurologists (the physicians and surgeons who deal with disorders of the brain and the nervous system).

Common disorders these specialists are often called on to treat include problems of deafness, tonsillitis, sinusitis, and head and neck cancers. In the surgical area, ENT specialists rely on a variety of surgical methods, including microsurgery, laser surgery, plastic surgery, and other reconstructive types of surgery. Thus specialists in this field must have a vast fund of knowledge of how and when to use various kinds of surgery and skills.

But the lines of responsibility are sometimes blurred in this area, and ENT specialists may be in competition with plastic surgeons and other specialists in allergy and pulmonary medicine.

This is a very competitive specialty requiring one or two years in general surgery followed by a fellowship of three to four years in ENT. Additional training is offered in such subspecialties as facial cosmetic and reconstructive surgery, otologic surgery, pediatric otolaryngology, and head and neck surgery.

Sponsoring organizations are the American Board of Otolaryngology, American College of Surgeons, and AMA Council on Medical Education.

PATHOLOGY

The pathologist's responsibilities are basically to find out, through various tests—blood chemistry, urinalysis, and others, as well as analysis of organ tissue—if a person is relatively healthy or ill or if an organ is healthy or diseased. In the latter case pathologists take a tiny slice of a tumor or part of an organ removed surgically and examine it under a microscope to see if it is cancerous or not.

In forensic pathology, a branch of the profession, the pathologist is called on to conduct autopsies to determine cause and time of death in cases where the death is in question.

Besides this there is the entire field of blood chemistry where the pathologists analyze blood samples or supervise technicians who analyze the samples for such things as white and red cells, corpuscles, platelets, cholesterol, and fatty substances to see if the patient is ill or not.

In his or her job as an investigator, the pathologist is a kind of doctor's detective, helping the physician to understand if tissue is cancerous or if infection is present in a patient, and then helping to work out a diagnosis as to the cause and treatment of same.

In this branch of medicine, the hours are fairly normal and life is low key. There is little of the pressure that characterizes most branches of medicine.

If you like people or want to build long-term, deep, and satisfying relationships with patients, then pathology is not for you, because patient contact is almost nil. But you will be working with other physicians, sometimes very closely, and with technicians and other professional personnel on various medical problems.

This is almost entirely a hospital-based specialty, since most pathologists direct the operation of the hospital's clinical laboratory as well as perform their own special duties in pathology. Although pathologists' earnings have been good in the past, averaging more than $210,000 in 1994, the enactment of the proposed Resource Based Relative Value Scale may see pathologists' earnings drop sharply.

Technological advancement in this field has been considerable and has resulted in the establishment of several subspecialties, including the above-mentioned forensic pathology.

Other subspecialties include blood banking, in which the specialist is responsible for maintaining an adequate blood supply for the hospital, for safeguarding blood donors and blood recipients, and for making sure the blood is used properly.

Chemical pathology deals with the body's biochemistry in relation to the cause and progress of disease. Often the chemical pathologist is a consultant in the diagnosis and treatment of disease.

Cytopathology studies body and organ cells to form diagnoses of various disorders. Cells are studied using special stains and chemical analyses.

Dermatopathology specialists diagnose and analyze diseases of the skin.

Hematology focuses on diseases that affect the bone marrow, lymph nodes, and above all the blood cells and the blood clotting systems.

Immunopathology involves applying immunological principles to the analysis of cells, tissue, and body fluids; the pathologist attempts to determine, among others, the prognosis or outlook of a given disease.

Medical microbiology provides pathologists' expertise in identifying and isolating microbes that can cause infectious disease.

Neuropathology involves analysis and diagnosis of diseases of the nervous and muscular systems.

Finally, there is pediatric pathology, in which the pathologist lends his or her other skills in the diagnosis of diseases affecting fetuses, infants, and children as they develop.

Jobs for pathologists are estimated to be reaching the saturation point, although there are still considerable openings due to pathologists reaching the retirement age.

In most of the more than 450 programs available, training involves five years of work in either clinical or anatomic pathology following completion of an internship in clinical medicine.

Sponsoring organizations include the American Board of Pathology, College of American Pathologists, and AMA Council on Medical Education.

PEDIATRICS

Pediatrics focuses on the study of diseases in infants and children, although in recent years this specialist's area of responsibility has been expanded to include adolescents.

Because of the nature of the practice, the pediatrician must have not only the vast knowledge required to treat the array of diseases and ailments presented, but a special understanding of, patience with, and affection for his or her young charges to be able to withstand the pressures of dealing with anxious parents and sick or ailing youngsters.

Today, due to a vast number of advances achieved in recent decades, the emphasis is on healthy children. Indeed today most pediatricians stress care of well babies and preventive medicine in the form of proper nutrition, rest, and inoculation, among others.

Diseases that pediatricians commonly see include developmental and behavioral problems, infectious diseases such as mumps and whooping cough, respiratory and throat diseases and ear infections, and congenital abnormalities.

Because children are prone to becoming ill at any time of the day or night, pediatricians often work long days and are subject to many interruptions in their personal lives.

The average pediatrician puts in a 58.6 hour workweek, spending 65 percent of the time in the office, 19 percent in the hospital, and 3 percent in surgical and other procedures. As a primary care physician working primarily in cognitive or diagnostic procedures to treat the ailments presented, the pediatrician is in the lower bracket in salaries received, averaging about $125,000 a year before taxes. Women currently comprise more than half of the number of pediatric residents.

The basic residency in the more than 600 programs available is for three years, after which the pediatrician can pursue fellowships involving additional training in several subspecialties as listed below.

Adolescent medicine.   Specialists in this area of medicine are trained in the unique physical, psychological, and social characteristics of adolescents, their health care problems, and their needs.

Clinical and laboratory immunology.   Here the specialist uses laboratory tests and complex procedures to diagnose and treat disorders of children's immune systems.

Medical toxicology.   A pediatric medical toxicologist focuses on the treatment and care of children who have been exposed to poisoning through the use of or abuse of drugs, household or industrial toxins, and other poisonous substances.

Neonatal-perinatal pediatrics.   The branch of pediatrics dealing with the care of infants and high-risk newborns.

Pediatric cardiology.   The specialty that offers complete cardiovascular care from fetus to young adult.

Pediatric critical care medicine.   The pediatrician who focuses on advanced life support for children from term or near term to adolescent.

Pediatric emergency medicine.   The pediatrician qualified to treat and manage emergencies in infants and children.

Pediatric endocrinology.   A pediatric specialist in the care of children and infants with disorders resulting from abnormalities of glands that secrete hormones.

Pediatric gastroenterology.   The focus of this children's specialist is on disorders of the digestive system of infants, children, and adolescents.

Pediatric hematology-oncology.   A pediatric specialist trained in diagnosis and treatment of blood disorders and cancer diseases in children.

Pediatric infectious diseases.   More than 20 percent of all children seen by the pediatrician suffer from some form of infectious diseases, and this specialist is involved with the management and care of children with problems involving infectious disease.

Pediatric nephrology.   Specialists who deal with children's diseases of the urinary tract or kidneys.

Pediatric pulmonology.   A specialist in respiratory diseases affecting children and infants.

Pediatric rheumatology.   This specialist is concerned with the prevention, identification, and treatment of rheumatic and related diseases of infants and children.

Sports medicine.   This specialist is concerned with the health care of children with medical problems involving exercise and recreational competitive sports.

PHYSICAL MEDICINE AND REHABILITATION

Known as physiatrists, these physicians specialize in the diagnosis and treatment of patients with muscular, neurologic, cardiovascular, and other body impairments and disorders. Here the object is to restore the patient's physical, mental, and social well-being through various methods or modalities of treatment.

A relatively new field, the practice, primarily hospital-based, involves helping to restore stroke and accident patients to health or helping patients suffering from a variety of neurological disorders, such as multiple sclerosis and Guillain-Barré disease, to maximize their lives and ability to function.

A broad knowledge of orthopedics, neurology, psychiatry, urology, and geriatrics is called for in this field. Contact with patients is common and hours are fairly regular. These specialists also treat disorders involving arthritis, lower-back pain, and head and spinal cord trauma. Training, offered in 80 programs, involves three years in physical medicine following completion of a one-year residency in internal medicine. The outlook is for a continuing need for specialists in this field for the foreseeable future.

Sponsoring organizations are the American Board of Physical Medicine and Rehabilitation, American Academy of Physical Medicine and Rehabilitation, and AMA Council on Medical Education.

PLASTIC SURGERY

This is perhaps the most glamorous branch of surgery, with some of these specialists involved in helping show business, sports, and other celebrities to get rid of unwanted wrinkles and blemishes and to make their noses and facial features more attractive. Even so, most plastic surgeons are involved in more mundane activities, such as helping victims of burns and accidents and those with birth defects to be restored to a more attractive appearance and to resume normal functions of the limbs.

Besides rhinoplasty, or nose restoration, plastic surgeons treat many other disabilities or disfigurements, such as congenital deformities (scars, lesions, birthmarks, and other disfigurements), facial trauma, cancer, and degenerative diseases. And in their work they use many new surgical treatments, such as liposuction for thighs and microsurgery.

Night work is often encountered in this field, with many plastic surgeons being called on to treat victims of burns, gunshot wounds, or automobile accidents.

As a result, much of the work is done on an ambulatory, or outpatient, basis. A sense of the artistic, which calls on one's aesthetic ability to visualize, is called for.

The field offers a good deal of satisfaction in that practitioners are often able to accomplish marked improvement in the patient's appearance. On the other hand, the plastic surgeon may encounter one of the major hazards of the practice—the patients' often unrealistic expectations of what the surgeon can do to make them look better. Consequently, this specialty is one of those areas in medicine most prone to malpractice suits, with resultant prohibitive costs to obtain insurance coverage. At the same time, earnings of practitioners are among the highest of all in medicine, with individual doctors averaging $219,000 a year.

This is a very competitive field with some surplus of specialists foreseen for the near future. It takes two to three years of general surgery followed by two to three years of training in plastic surgery to qualify for certification.

In most cases plastic surgeons obtain their patients through referrals and patient contacts are limited to visits prior to and after surgery.

Sponsoring organizations include the American Board of Plastic Surgeons, American College of Surgeons, American Society of Plastic and Reconstructive Surgeons, and AMA Council on Medical Education.

PREVENTIVE MEDICINE

This is the branch of medicine that strives through public education and media exposure to help people to live their lives as fully and completely as possible by eliminating unnecessary public hazards—such as environmental health hazards and illness due to smoking and alcoholism.

Those wishing to specialize in this field have three main routes to certification: aerospace medicine, occupational or industrial medicine, and public health medicine. A broad background in epidemiology, health education and policy, nutrition, and health services administration and management is required for certification.

Most specialists in preventive medicine hold positions in public health agencies at the local, state, or federal levels or are attached to the armed forces or private industry. Besides completing all of the courses required for certification, applicants in this field are required to have a Masters of Public Health degree or the equivalent.

Aerospace medicine. Many specialists in this field are or were in the armed forces and work with pilots or flight crews. The focus is on maintaining the health of passengers, flight crews, and support personnel on air and space vehicles. Training consists of a year's internship followed by at least two years of residency, one of which must be in public health medicine, and completion of the requirements for a master's degree in public health.

There are three training programs in the military, and applicants must be in the service and practicing as flight surgeons to be considered.

Occupational medicine. Specialists in this field often practice in industry, government, teaching hospitals, or occupational health clinics. The focus is on preventing occupational and industrial hazards, such as air or water pollution, exposure to radiation, and hazards of either the workplace or the community. Night call is rare as is responsibility for treating hospitalized patients. Training in some 26 programs consists of two to three years of residency upon completion of a year's internship. A fourth year in public health practice, teaching, or research is required for certification. A shortage of practitioners is foreseen for this specialty in the immediate future.

Public health and general preventive medicine. This is the route to preventive health medicine that is most involved in public health and public awareness programs, including maternal health, inoculation programs and AIDS alert programs. Specialists are involved in community health problems arising from such factors as environmental hazards, epidemics of one kind or other, smoking, and other risks. They do not treat individual patients.

The object is to gain information on the level of public health in the community, and based on this information, to develop programs aimed at eliminating or lessening community health hazards. Training involves completion of at least two years of residency, including a year of public health, following completion of an internship.

Currently 28 programs in allopathic medicine and one in osteopathic medicine offer training in this area. In addition, the preventive medicine specialist can go on to be certified in two subspecialties: medical toxicology and undersea medicine. Medical toxicology is the management of patients poisoned through exposure to medications, drugs, household or industrial toxins, and environmental toxins.

The undersea medicine specialist is required to have one additional year of residency training to qualify for specialization in treating diseases caused by barometric pressure higher or lower than normal atmospheric pressure.

Sponsoring organizations include the American Board of Preventive Medicine, and AMA Council of Medical Education.

PSYCHIATRY

Psychiatrists treat and diagnose disorders of the mind. The scope of mental problems ranges from situation disturbances involving family or friends to problems of chemical imbalances to severe psychiatric disorders such as schizophrenia or dementia. In the past psychiatrists have used various types of therapy to treat patients, including hydrotherapy (immersion in water tanks), psychotherapy (practiced primarily by followers of Sigmund Freud and his associates), and shock treatment. Today, however, the emphasis is on psychotropic medications, which are very effective and which have given the psychiatrist an arsenal of drugs that he or she can use in controlling mental disease. Psychiatrists practice in a variety of settings. They work primarily out of their own offices, but they also are attached to community health centers, psychiatric and short-term care hospitals (which treat primarily short-term acute disorders), and substance abuse centers.

Perhaps more so than almost every other medical specialty psychiatry is people-oriented, and specialists must see things from the patient's perspective—get into the patient's mind, so to speak. Although many conditions are chronic and debilitating over a period of years, psychiatrists nevertheless can contribute a good deal, through their understanding and support, to make life a little better and more fulfilling for both patients and their families. Quite often they can help patients with mental problems stemming from physical problems (psychosomatic medicine) and short-term illnesses such as alcoholism or drug abuse, to regain their balance and continue as normal, functioning human beings.

Hours are for the most part fairly regular, but salaries, whether you are in practice or attached to a private clinic, are on the low side, averaging $108,000 in 1994. Training consists of a year's internship followed by three years in psychiatry with a heavy neurological component, because many psychiatric disorders are rooted in neurological problems that affect the brain.

Currently more than 300 residency programs offer training in this field. Sponsoring organizations include the American Board of Psychiatry, American Psychiatric Association, and AMA Council on Medical Education.

With one to two years of additional training, psychiatrists can be certified in several subspecialties:

Addiction psychiatry.   This subspecialty deals with addictive disorders and special emotional problems related to addiction and substance abuse.

Child and adolescent psychiatry.   A psychiatry subspecialty that focuses on mental, addictive, and emotional disorders of children.

Clinical neurophysiology.   Central and peripheral nervous system disorders are the concern of this specialist, who uses a variety of electrophysiological techniques.

Forensic psychiatry.   A psychiatric specialist with skills in diagnosing patients with sexual, antisocial personality, and paranoid disorders.

Geriatric psychiatry.   This specialist understands the special needs of the elderly in the diagnosis and treatment of their mental disorders and hangups.

PULMONARY MEDICINE

Pulmonary medicine, another subspecialty of internal medicine, focuses on diseases of the lungs and the respiratory system.

Specialists in this field are concerned with such diseases as cancer, occupational disease, emphysema, and pneumonia. Although pulmonary specialists see many patients in the office, a good part of their time is spent in the hospital treating the complications of various lung diseases.

Patients are usually obtained through physician referrals or word of mouth. Hours are fairly normal, but due to emergencies, they can be very long as well. Training in the approximately 73 programs in this specialty and 73 in pulmonary critical care disease consists of a two- or three-year fellowship in pulmonary medicine following a three-year residency in internal medicine.

Sponsoring organizations include the American Board of Internal Medicine, American College of Chest Physicians, and AMA Council on Medical Education.

RADIOLOGY

Radiologists are specialists who deal with the use of radioactive substances and equipment to treat and diagnose disease. Formerly specialists in this branch of medicine did both functions themselves—treatment of patients and diagnosis of disease—but in recent years the specialty has become so broad that they have been split into two subspecialties.

Radiological oncology.   Basically therapists in this subspecialty use sophisticated equipment in treating malignancies and other diseases. A rapidly evolving specialty, this field now covers such complex equipment as cobalt treatment centers and radiographic treatment of malignancies.

As new technology is developed, the field is constantly expanding, and these specialists must spend a good deal of time keeping abreast of new developments. Training, which consists of a year's internship, is followed by three years of specialized training in radiation oncology.

Diagnostic radiology.   The bulk of the more than 24,000 radiologists are involved in this area of radiology, which through complex X-ray and other imaging equipment helps supply the data and photos that physicians need to arrive at a diagnosis of the particular problem involved.

Equipment and procedures, which are highly technical and which are constantly evolving, include MRI (Magnetic Resonance Imaging), CT (Computerized Tomography) Scanners, and PET (Positive Emissions Tomography), as well as radioactive isotopes (nuclear medicine) and ultrasound. Primarily the radiologist is a consultant to the referring physician in interpreting X-ray film and the results of various tests undertaken. The range of problems is as broad as medicine itself and includes fractures, gastric disorders, cardiovascular diseases, pulmonary diseases, and many other disorders.

Operating mostly behind the scenes, usually on a one-time basis with most patients, radiologists seldom, if ever, develop long-term relationships with patients. However, they do work closely with referring physicians and their own staffs of technicians and nurses.

Training in this specialty involves four years of residency following completion of an internship. In 1994 there were 206 programs in diagnostic radiology and 83 in radiation oncology.

With additional training, radiologists can be certified in several subspecialties:

Radiological physics. This specialty deals with the diagnostic and therapeutic application of X-rays, gamma rays from sealed sources, ultrasound, and radio-frequency radiation.

Neuroradiology. This subspecialty utilizes imaging procedures as they relate to the brain, spine and spinal cord, head, neck, and organs of special sense in patients.

Nuclear radiology. Here the specialist is concerned with the analysis and imaging of radionuclides and radiolabeled substances and the administration of radionuclides and radiolabeled substances for the treatment of disease.

Pediatric radiology. A radiologist with special skills in the imaging of disorders of newborns, infants, and children.

Vascular and interventional radiology. A specialist who diagnoses and treats disease by various invasive techniques guided by radiologic imaging including fluoroscopy, digital radiography, computed tomography sonography, and MRI.

RHEUMATOLOGY

This internal medicine subspecialty focuses on diseases of the joints, soft tissue, and blood vessels. Arthritis, back pain, and muscle, joint, and skeletal problems are all concerns of the rheumatologist.

One of the least stressful of the internal medicine subspecialties, rheumatology seldom involves night calls and emergencies. The field has expanded in recent years primarily because of the keen interest in autoimmune diseases, which underlie many rheumatological conditions.

As is true of many subspecialties in internal medicine, training involves completion of a two- to three-year fellowship in rheumatology upon completion of a three-year residency in internal medicine. Currently 121 programs offer training in this specialty.

Sponsoring organizations include the American Board of Internal Medicine and AMA Council on Medical Education.

THORACIC SURGERY

This is the branch of surgery that deals with diseases of the chest cavity—including the heart, arteries leading to the heart, aneurysm, and lung cancer. Perhaps more so than in any other kind of surgery, these practitioners need coolness under pressure and the ability to work swiftly, as well as manual dexterity and stamina. Because of their efforts, thoracic surgeons quite often see dramatic and swift changes for the better in their patient's health, thus the work can be very satisfying.

Although the income level is among the highest in all medicine, with salaries grossing an average of $265,000 in 1994, the expenses, particularly for malpractice coverage, are also high.

Symptomatic of the vast amount of knowledge and skill required for this specialty is the training period—the lengthiest in medicine—involving a five-year internship and residency in general surgery, followed by a two- to three-year fellowship in thoracic surgery. The field is very competitive, and a considerable surplus of practitioners is seen for the immediate future.

Sponsoring organizations include the American Board of Thoracic Surgery, Society of Thoracic Surgeons, and AMA Council on Medical Education.

UROLOGY

Working in a medical specialty that is both surgical and medical in approach, urologists specialize in diseases of the genito-urinary tract, which includes the kidneys, bladder, and urethra, and, in males, the prostate and the genitals.

With a considerable reliance on diagnostic techniques, urologists quite often use medical treatments—drugs primarily—to effect cures for their patients. Severity of conditions presented can range from mild and easily treated to very acute and uncomfortable.

Since conditions treated are often long-term, urologists can develop personal and satisfying relationships with their patients. The field is characterized by the development of considerable technology to help effect cures and positive results, such as shock wave lithotripsy (effective in dissolving kidney and gallstones), prostatic ultrasound, and endoscopic surgery. Besides a deep understanding of physiology and anatomy, urologists need exceptional manual dexterity and coordination.

The field pays well, averaging $230,000 in 1994, but training is lengthy. The 130 training programs available require a two-year residency and internship followed by three years in urology. Projections for estimated need of urologists see a considerable surplus in the immediate future.

Sponsoring organizations include the American Board of Urology, American Urological Association, and AMA Council on Medical Education.

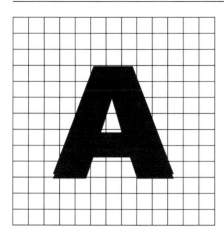

APPENDIX A
MEDICAL SCHOOLS IN THE UNITED STATES AND CANADA

U.S. SCHOOLS

Alabama
University of Alabama
School of Medicine
VH 100
Birmingham, AL 35294-0019

University of South Alabama
College of Medicine
Room 2015, Medical Sciences
    Building
Mobile, AL 36688-0002

Arizona
University of Arizona
College of Medicine
Tucson, AZ 85724

Arkansas
University of Arkansas
College of Medicine
4301 Markham Street
Little Rock, AR 72205-7199

California
Loma Linda University
School of Medicine
Loma Linda, CA 92350

Stanford University
School of Medicine
851 Welch Road, Room 154
Palo Alto, CA 94306-1677

University of California, Davis
School of Medicine
Davis, CA 95616

University of California, Irvine
School of Medicine
118 Medsurge I
Irvine, CA 92717-3952

University of California, Los Angeles
School of Medicine
Center for Health Sciences
Los Angeles, CA 90095-1720

University of California, San Diego
School of Medicine
9500 Gilman Drive
La Jolla, CA 92093-0621

University of California, San
    Francisco
School of Medicine
C-200, Box 0408
San Francisco, CA 94143

University of Southern California
School of Medicine
1975 Zonal Avenue
Los Angeles, CA 90033

Colorado
University of Colorado
School of Medicine
4200 East Ninth Avenue, C-297
Denver, CO 80262

Connecticut
University of Connecticut
School of Medicine
University of Connecticut Health
    Center
263 Farmington Avenue
Room AG-062
Farmington, CT 06030-1905

Yale University
School of Medicine
367 Cedar Street
New Haven, CT 06510

District of Columbia
George Washington University
School of Medicine and Health
    Sciences
2300 Eye Street, NW
Washington, DC 20037

Georgetown University
School of Medicine
3900 Reservoir Road, NW
Washington, DC 20007

Howard University
College of Medicine
520 W Street, NW
Washington, DC 20059

Florida
University of Florida
College of Medicine
Box 100216
J. Hillis Miller Health Center
Gainesville, FL 32610

University of Miami
School of Medicine
P.O. Box 016159
Miami, FL 33101

University of South Florida
College of Medicine
12901 Bruce B. Downs Boulevard
Tampa, FL 33612-4799

Georgia
Emory University
School of Medicine
Room 303, Woodruff Health Sciences
    Center
Atlanta, GA 30322-4510

Medical College of Georgia
Augusta, GA 30912-4760

Mercer University
School of Medicine
Macon, GA 31207

Morehouse School of Medicine
729 Westview Drive, SW
Atlanta, GA 30310-1495

Hawaii
University of Hawaii
John A. Burns School of Medicine
1960 East-West Boulevard
Honolulu, Hawaii 96822

Illinois
Loyola University
Stritch School of Medicine
2160 South First Avenue
Maywood, IL 60153

Northwestern University
Medical School
303 East Chicago Avenue
Chicago, IL 60611

Rush Medical College of Rush
    University
524 Academic Facility
600 South Paulina Street
Chicago, IL 60612

Southern Illinois University
School of Medicine
P.O. Box 19230
Springfield, IL 62794-9280

University of Chicago
Pritzker School of Medicine
924 East 57th Street
Chicago, IL 60637

University of Health Sciences
The Chicago Medical School
3333 Green Bay Road
North Chicago, IL 60064

University of Illinois
College of Medicine
Room 165 CME M/C 783
808 South Wood Street
Chicago, IL 60612-7302

Indiana
Indiana University
School of Medicine
Fesler Hall 213
120 South Drive
Indianapolis, IN 46202-5113

Iowa
University of Iowa
College of Medicine
100 Medicine Administration
  Building
Iowa City, IA 52242-1101

Kansas
University of Kansas
School of Medicine
3901 Rainbow Boulevard
Kansas City, KS 66160-7301

Kentucky
University of Kentucky
College of Medicine
Chandler Medical Center
800 Rose Street
Lexington, KY 40536-0084

University of Louisville
School of Medicine
Health Sciences Center
Louisville, KY 40292

Louisiana
Louisiana State University
School of Medicine in New Orleans
1901 Perdido Street
New Orleans, LA 70112-1393

Louisiana State University
School of Medicine in Shreveport
P.O. Box 33932
Shreveport, LA 71130-3932

Tulane University
School of Medicine
1430 Tulane Avenue
New Orleans, LA 70112-2699

Maryland
Johns Hopkins University
School of Medicine
720 Rutland Avenue
Baltimore, MD 21205-2196

Uniformed Services University of the
  Health Sciences
E. Edward Hebert School of Medicine
4301 Jones Bridge Road
Bethesda, MD 20814-4799

University of Maryland
School of Medicine
655 West Baltimore Street
Baltimore, MD 21201

Massachusetts
Boston University
School of Medicine
80 East Concord Street
Boston, MA 02118

Harvard Medical School
25 Shattuck Street
Room 210
Boston, MA 02115-6092

Tufts University
School of Medicine
136 Harrison Avenue, Stearns I
Boston, MA 02111

University of Massachusetts
Medical School
55 Lake Avenue
Worcester, MA 01655

Michigan
Michigan State University
College of Human Medicine
A-239 Life Sciences
East Lansing, MI 48824-1317

University of Michigan
Medical School
M4130 Medical Science I Building
Ann Arbor, MI 48109-0611

Wayne State University
School of Medicine
540 East Canfield
Detroit, MI 48201

Minnesota
Mayo Medical School
200 First Street, NW
Rochester, MN 55905

University of Minnesota-Duluth
School of Medicine
10 University Drive
Duluth, MN 55812

University of Minnesota-Minneapolis
Medical School
420 Delaware Street, SE
Minneapolis, MN 55455-0310

Mississippi
University of Mississippi
School of Medicine
2500 North State Street
Jackson, MS 39216-4505

Missouri
St. Louis University
School of Medicine
1402 South Grand Boulevard
St. Louis, MO 63104

University of Missouri-Columbia
School of Medicine
MA202 Medical Sciences Building
One Hospital Drive
Columbia, MO 65212

University of Missouri-Kansas City
School of Medicine
2411 Holmes
Kansas City, MO 64108

Washington University
School of Medicine
660 South Euclid Avenue #8107
St. Louis, MO 63110

Nebraska
Creighton University
School of Medicine
2500 California Plaza
Omaha, NE 68178

University of Nebraska
College of Medicine
Room 4004 Conkling Hall
600 South Forty-second Street
Omaha, NE 68198-4430

Nevada
University of Nevada
School of Medicine
Mail Stop 357
Reno, NV 89557

New Hampshire
Dartmouth Medical School
7020 Remsen, Room 306
Hanover, NH 03755-3833

New Jersey
University of Medicine and Dentistry
    of New Jersey
New Jersey Medical School
185 South Orange Street
Newark, NJ 07103

University of Medicine and Dentistry
    of New Jersey
Robert Wood Johnson Medical School
675 Hoes Lane
Piscataway, NJ 08854-5635

New Mexico
University of New Mexico
School of Medicine
Basic Medical Sciences Building,
Room 107
Albuquerque, NM 87131-5166

New York
Albany Medical College of Union
University
47 New Scotland Avenue
Albany, NY 12208

Albert Einstein College of Medicine
of Yeshiva University
Jack and Pearl Resnick Campus
1300 Morris Park Avenue
Bronx, NY 10461

Columbia University College of
Physicians and Surgeons
Admissions Office, Room 1-416
630 West 168th Street
New York, NY 10032

Cornell University
Medical College
445 East Sixty-ninth Street
New York, NY 10021

Mt. Sinai School of Medicine of the
City University of New York
Annenberg Building, Room S-04
One Gustave I. Levy Place
Box 1002
New York, NY 10029-6574

New York Medical College
Room 127, Sunshine Cottage
Valhalla, NY 10595

New York University
School of Medicine
P.O. Box 1924
New York, NY 10016

State University of New York
Health Science Center at Brooklyn
College of Medicine
450 Clarkson Avenue, Box 60M
Brooklyn, NY 11203

State University of New York at
Buffalo
School of Medicine
CFS Building, Room 35
Buffalo, NY 14214-3013

State University of New York at Stony
Brook
Health Sciences Center School of
Medicine, Level 4, Room 147
Stony Brook, NY 11794-8434

State University of New York
Health Science Center at Syracuse
College of Medicine
155 Elizabeth Blackwell Street
Syracuse, NY 13210

University of Rochester
School of Medicine and Dentistry
Medical Center Box 601
Rochester, NY 14642

North Carolina
Bowman Gray School of Medicine of
Wake Forest University
Medical Center Boulevard
Winston-Salem, NC 27857-1090

Duke University
School of Medicine
Duke University Medical Center
P.O. Box 3710
Durham, NC 27710

East Carolina University
School of Medicine
Greenville, NC 27858-4354

University of North Carolina at
Chapel Hill
School of Medicine
CBH 7000 MacNider Hall
Chapel Hill, NC 27599-7000

North Dakota
University of North Dakota
School of Medicine
501 North Columbia Road
Box 9037
Grand Forks, ND 58202-9037

Ohio
Case Western Reserve University
School of Medicine
10900 Euclid Avenue
Cleveland, OH 44106-4920

Medical College of Ohio at Toledo
P.O. Box 10008
Toledo, OH 43699

Northeastern Ohio Universities
College of Medicine
P.O. Box 95
Rootstown, OH 44272-0095

Ohio State University
College of Medicine
270-A Meiling Hall
370 West Ninth Avenue
Columbus, OH 43210-1238

University of Cincinnati
College of Medicine
P.O. Box 670552
Cincinnati, OH 45267-0552

Wright State University
School of Medicine
P.O. Box 1751
Dayton, OH 45401

Oklahoma
University of Oklahoma
College of Medicine
P.O. Box 26901
Oklahoma City, OK 73190

Oregon
Oregon Health Sciences
University School of Medicine
3181 SW Sam Jackson Park Road
Portland, OR 97201

Pennsylvania
Jefferson Medical College of Thomas
    Jefferson University
1025 Walnut Street
Philadelphia, PA 19107

Medical College of Pennsylvania and
    Hahnemann University
College of Medicine
2900 Queenlane Avenue
Philadelphia, PA 19129

Pennsylvania State University
College of Medicine
P.O. Box 850
Hershey, PA 17033

Temple University
School of Medicine
Suite 305, Student Faculty Center
Broad and Ontario Streets
Philadelphia, PA 19140

University of Pennsylvania
School of Medicine
Edward J. Stemmler Hall, Suite 100
Philadelphia, PA 19104-6056

University of Pittsburgh
School of Medicine
518 Scaife Hall
Pittsburgh PA 15261

Puerto Rico
Ponce School of Medicine
P.O. Box 7004
Ponce, Puerto Rico 00732

Universidad Central del Caribe
School of Medicine
Ramon Ruiz Armau University
    Hospital
Call Box 60-327
Bayamon, Puerto Rico 00621-6032

University of Puerto Rico
School of Medicine
Medical Sciences Campus
P.O. Box 365067
San Juan, Puerto Rico 00936-5067

Rhode Island
Brown University
Program in Medicine
97 Waterman Street, Box GA212
Providence, RI 02912-9706

South Carolina
Medical University of South Carolina
College of Medicine
171 Ashley Avenue
Charleston, SC 29425

University of South Carolina
School of Medicine
Columbia, SC 29208

South Dakota
University of South Dakota
School of Medicine
414 East Clark Street
Vermillion, SD 57069-2390

Tennessee
East Tennessee State University
James H. Quillen College of Medicine
P.O. Box 70580
Johnson City, TN 37614-0580

Meharry Medical College
School of Medicine
1005 D.B. Todd, Jr. Boulevard
Nashville, TN 37208

University of Tennessee
Memphis College of Medicine
790 Madison Street
Memphis, TN 38163-2166

Vanderbilt University
School of Medicine
Nashville, TN 37232-0685

Texas
Baylor College of Medicine
One Baylor Place
Houston, TX 77030

Texas A&M University
College of Medicine
College Station, TX 77843-1114

Texas Tech University Health Sciences
   Center
School of Medicine
Lubbock, TX 79430

University of Texas
Southwestern Medical Center at
   Dallas School of Medicine
5323 Harry Hines Boulevard
Dallas, TX 75235-9096

University of Texas
Medical School at Galveston
School of Medicine
Galveston, TX 77444-1317

University of Texas
Houston Medical School
P.O. Box 20708
Houston, TX 77225

University of Texas
Medical School of San Antonio
Health Science Center at San Antonio
7703 Floyd Curl Drive
San Antonio, TX 78284-7701

Utah
University of Utah
School of Medicine
50 North Medical Drive
Salt Lake City, UT 84132

Vermont
University of Vermont
College of Medicine
Burlington, VT 05405

Virginia
Eastern Virginia Medical
   School of the Medical
   College of Hampton Roads
721 Fairfax Avenue
Norfolk, VA 23507-2000

Virginia Commonwealth University
Medical College of Virginia
MCV Station, Box 98065
Richmond, VA 23298-0565

University of Virginia
School of Medicine
Charlottesville, VA 22908

Washington
University of Washington
School of Medicine
Health Sciences Center A-300
Seattle, WA 98195

West Virginia
Marshall University
School of Medicine
1542 Spring Valley Drive
Huntington, WV 25704

West Virginia University
School of Medicine
Health Sciences Center
P.O. Box 9815
Morgantown, WV 26506

Wisconsin
Medical College of Wisconsin
8701 Watertown Plank Road
Milwaukee, WI 53226

University of Wisconsin
Medical School
Medical Sciences Center, Room 1250
1300 University Avenue
Madison, WI 53706

CANADIAN MEDICAL SCHOOLS

Alberta
University of Alberta
Faculty of Medicine
2-45 Medical Sciences Building
Edmonton, Alberta T6G 2H7

University of Calgary
Faculty of Medicine
3330 Hospital Drive NW
Calgary, Alberta T2N 4N1

British Columbia
University of British Columbia
Faculty of Medicine
317-2194 Health Sciences Mall
Vancouver, British Columbia
   V6T 1Z3

Manitoba
University of Manitoba
Faculty of Medicine
753 McDermot Avenue
Winnipeg, Manitoba R3E 0W3

Newfoundland
Memorial University of
   Newfoundland
Faculty of Medicine
St. John's, Newfoundland A1B 3V6

Nova Scotia
Dalhousie University
Faculty of Medicine
5849 University Avenue
Halifax, Nova Scotia B3H 4H7

Ontario
McMaster University
Faculty of Medicine
1200 Main Street West
Hamilton, Ontario L8N 3Z5

University of Ottawa
Faculty of Medicine
451 Smyth Road
Ottawa, Ontario K1H 8M5

Queen's University
Faculty of Medicine
Kingston, Ontario K7L 3N6

University of Toronto
Faculty of Medicine
Toronto, Ontario M5S 1A8

University of Western Ontario
Faculty of Medicine
London, Ontario N6A SC1

Quebec

Université Laval
Faculty of Medicine
Ste.-Foy, Quebec G1K 7P4

McGill University
Faculty of Medicine
3655 Drummond Street
Montreal, Quebec H3G 1Y6

University of Montreal
Faculty of Medicine
P.O. Box 6128, Station Centreville
Montreal, Quebec H3C 3J7

University of Sherbrooke
Faculty of Medicine
Sherbrooke, Quebec J1H 5N4

Saskatchewan

University of Saskatchewan
College of Medicine
Saskatoon, Saskatchewan S7N 0W0

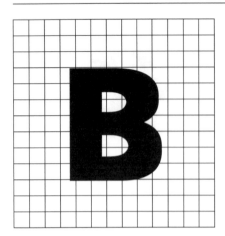

MEDICAL ORGANIZATIONS AND SPECIALTY BOARDS

MEDICAL ORGANIZATIONS

Aerospace Medical Association
320 South Henry Street
Alexandria, VA 22314

American Academy of Allergy and
  Immunology
611 East Wells Street
Milwaukee, WI 53202

American Academy of Child and
  Adolescent Psychiatry
3615 Wisconsin Street, NW
Washington, DC 20016

American Academy of Dermatology
930 Meacham Road
Schaumburg, IL 60172-4965

American Academy of Family
  Physicians
8880 Ward Parkway
Kansas City, MO 64114-2797

American Academy of Neurology
2221 University Avenue, SE
Suite 335
Minneapolis, MN 55414

American Academy of
  Ophthalmology
655 Beach Street
P.O. Box 7424
San Francisco, CA 94109

American Academy of Orthopaedic
  Surgeons
6300 North River Road
Rosemont, IL 60018-4226

American Academy of Pediatrics
141 Northwest Point Boulevard
P.O. Box 927
Elk Grove Village, IL 60009-0927

American Academy of Physical
  Medicine and Rehabilitation
1 IBM Plaza - 25th Floor
Chicago, IL 60611-3604

American Association of Neurological
  Surgeons
22 South Washington Street
Suite 100
Park Ridge, IL 60068

American Board of Medical
 Specialties
1007 Church Street
Suite 404
Evanston, IL 60201-5913

American College of Allergy &
 Immunology
85 West Algonquin Road, Suite 550
Arlington Heights, IL 60005

American College of Cardiology
9111 Old Georgetown Road
Bethesda, MD 20815-1699

American College of Chest Physicians
3300 Dundee Road
Northbrook, IL 60062

American College of Colon & Rectal
 Surgery
615 Griswold, Suite 1717
Detroit, MI 48226

American College of Emergency
 Physicians
P.O. Box 75261-9911
Dallas, TX 75261-9911

American College of
 Gastroenterologists
4900 B S 31st Street
Arlington, VA 22206

American College of Physicians
Independence Mall West
6th Street at Race
Philadelphia, PA 19106

American College of Preventive
 Medicine
1015 Fifteenth Street, NW
Washington, DC 20005

American College of Radiology
1891 Preston White Drive
Reston, VA 22091

American College of Rheumatism
60 Executive Park S - Suite 150
Atlanta, GA 30329

American College of Surgeons
55 East Erie Street
Chicago, IL 60611

American College Testing Program
P.O. Box 4056
Iowa City, IA 52243

American Council for Graduate
 Medical Education
535 North Dearborn Street
Chicago, IL 60610

American Geriatrics Society
770 Lexington Avenue, Suite 400
New York, NY 10021

American Medical Association
515 North State Street
Chicago, IL 60610-0174

American Medical College
 Application Service (AMCAS)
Association of American Medical
 Colleges
2450 N Street, NW, Suite 201
Washington, DC 20037-1131

American Medical Student
 Association
1902 Association Drive
Reston, VA 22091

American Medical Women
 Association
801 North Fairfax Street
Arlington, VA 22314

American Osteopathic Association
142 East Ontario Street
Chicago, IL 60611-2864

American Psychiatric Association
1400 K Street, NW
Washington, DC 20005

American Society of
 Anesthesiologists
520 North Northwest Highway
Park Ridge, IL 60068-2573

American Society of Clinical
  Oncology
435 North Michigan Avenue
Suite 1717
Chicago, IL 60611-4067

American Society for Colon and
  Rectal Surgery
85 West Algonquin Road
Suite 550
Arlington Heights, IL 60005

American Society of Hematology
1101 Connecticut Avenue, NW
7th Floor
Washington, DC 20036-4303

American Society for Internal
  Medicine
2011 Pennsylvania Avenue, NW
Suite 800
Washington, DC 20006-1808

American Society of Nephrology
1200 - 19th Street, NW
Washington, DC 20036

American Society of Plastic and
  Reconstructive Surgeons
444 East Algonquin Road
Arlington Heights, IL 60005

American Thoracic Society
1740 Broadway
New York, NY 10019-4374

American Urological Association
1120 North Charles Street
Baltimore, MD 21201

Association of American Medical
  Colleges
2450 N Street, NW
Washington, DC 20037

Association of Canadian Medical
  Colleges
774 Echo Drive
Ottawa, Ontario
Canada K1S 5P2

Canadian Medical Association
P.O. Box CP8650
1867 Alta Vista Street
Ottawa, Ontario
Canada K16 346

College of American Pathologists
325 Waukegan Road
Northfield, IL 60093-2750

Endocrine Society
9650 Rockville Pike
Bethesda, MD 20814

Infectious Diseases Society of
  America
1200 - 19th Street, NW
Suite 300
Washington, DC 20036-2401

Medical College Admission Test
  (MCAT)
c/o American College Testing
  Program
P.O. Box 4056
Iowa City, IA 52243

National Board of Medical Examiners
3930 Chestnut Street
Philadelphia, PA 19104

National Medical Association
1012 Tenth Avenue, NW
Washington, DC 20001

National Resident Matching Program
2450 N Street, NW
Suite 201
Washington, DC 20037-1141

Radiological Society of North
  America
2021 Spring Road - Suite 600
Oak Brook, IL 60521

Renal Physicians Association
2011 Pennsylvania Avenue, NW
Suite 800
Washington, DC 20006-1808

Society of Critical Care Medicine
8101 East Kaiser Boulevard
Anaheim, CA 92808-2259

Society of Thoracic Surgeons
401 North Michigan Avenue
Chicago, IL 60611-4267

Society for Vascular Surgery
13 Elm Street
P.O. Box 1564
Manchester, MA 01944

SPECIALTY BOARDS

American Board of Allergy and
    Immunology
University City Science Center
3624 Market Street
Philadelphia, PA 19104-2675

American Board of Anesthesiology
100 Constitution Plaza
Hartford, CT 06103-1796

American Board of Colon and Rectal
    Surgery
20600 Eureka Road
Suite 713
Taylor, MI 48180

American Board of Dermatology
Henry Ford Hospital
Ford Place
Detroit, MI 48202-3450

American Board of Emergency
    Medicine
3000 Coolidge Road
East Lansing, MI 48823

American Board of Family Practice
2228 Young Drive
Lexington, KY 40505

American Board of Internal Medicine
University City Science Center
3624 Market Street
Philadelphia, PA 19104-2675

American Board of Medical Genetics
9650 Rockville Pike
Bethesda, MD 20814-3998

American Board of Neurological
    Surgery
Smith Tower, Suite 2139
6550 Fanning Street
Houston, TX 17030-2701

American Board of Nuclear Medicine
900 Veteran Avenue, Room 12-200
Los Angeles, CA 90024-1786

American Board of Obstetrics and
    Gynecology
2915 Vine Street
Dallas, TX 75204

American Board of Ophthalmology
111 Presidential Boulevard
Suite 241
Bala Cynwyd, PA 19004

American Board of Orthopaedic
    Surgeons
400 Silver Cedar Court
Chapel Hill, NC 27514

American Board of Otolaryngology
5615 Kirby Drive, Suite 936
Houston, TX 77005

American Board of Pathology
P.O. Box 24915
Tampa, FL 33622-5915

American Board of Pediatrics
111 Silver Cedar Court
Chapel Hill, NC 27514-1651

American Board of Physical Medicine
and Rehabilitation
Suite 674, Northwest Center
21 First Street, NW
Rochester, MN 55902

American Board of Plastic Surgery
1635 Market Street
Philadelphia, PA 19103-2204

American Board of Preventive
Medicine
9950 West Lawrence Avenue
Suite 106
Schiller Park, IL 60176

American Board of Psychiatry and
Neurology
500 Lake Cook Road, #335
Deerfield, IL 60015

American Board of Radiology
5255 East Williams Circle
Suite 6800
Tucson, AZ 85711

American Board of Surgery
1617 John F. Kennedy Boulevard
Suite 860
Philadelphia, PA 19103-1847

American Board of Thoracic Surgery
One Rotary Center, Suite 803
Evanston, IL 60201

American Board of Urology
31700 Telegraph Road
Suite 150
Bingham Farms, MI 48025

APPENDIX C
BIBLIOGRAPHY

CAREERS IN MEDICINE

Bleich, Alan R. *Exploring Careers in Medicine*. New York: Rosen Publishing Group, rev. 1988.

Davis, W. K., C. Colon, *et al.* "Medical Career Choice: Current Status of Research Literature." *Teaching and Learning in Medicine*, 2(3):130–35.

Farr, J. Michael. *America's Top Medical and Human Services Jobs*. Washington, DC: U.S. Department of Labor, 1995.

"The Future of Cardiology." *Journal of the American Medical Association*, 262:20:2874–78, 1988.

"The Future of Family Practice." *Journal of the American Medical Association*, 260:9:1272–79, 1988.

"The Future of General Internal Medicine." *Journal of the American Medical Association*, 262:15:2119–24, 1988.

"The Future of General Surgery." *Journal of the American Medical Association*, 262:22:3178–83, 1988.

"The Future of Obstetrics and Gynecology." *Journal of the American Medical Association*, 258:24:3574–53, 1987.

"The Future of Pathology." *Journal of the American Medical Association*, 258:24:3547–53, 1987.

"The Future of Pediatrics." *Journal of the American Medical Association*, 258:2:240–45, 1987.

Got That Feeling. Washington, DC: Division of Communications, Association of American Medical Colleges, and Chicago: Division of Undergraduate Education. The American Medical Association.

Marmon, J. "Psychiatrists are Prone to Depression." *American Medical News*, 26(18):14, 1982.

McCauley, M. H. *Application of the Myers-Briggs Type Indicator to Medicine and Other Health Professions*. Gainesville, FL: Center for Applications of Psychological Type, Inc. 1978, pp. 253–54.

Medicine: A Chance to Make a Difference. Washington, DC: Association of American Medical Colleges, Division of Communications, and Chicago: Division of Undergraduate Education, American Medical Association.

Medicine as a Career. Chicago: Division of Undergraduate Education, American Medical Association, 515 North State Street, Chicago, IL 60610.

"Physicians." *Occupational Outlook Handbook*, Washington, DC: Bureau of Labor Statistics, 1994–95.

Socioeconomic Fact Book for Surgery. Chicago: American College of Surgeons, 55 East Erie Street,Chicago, IL 60610.

Sugar-Webb, Jan. *Physician Careers*. Lincolnwood, IL: VGM Careers Horizons, NTC Publishing Group, 1990.

Wright, John W. "Doctors." *The American Almanac of Jobs and Salaries*, 1995.

CHOOSING A MEDICAL CAREER

Accreditation of Graduate Medical Educational Programs. Chicago: Accreditation Council for Graduate Medical Education, 535 North Dearborn Street, Chicago, IL 60619.

Colon and Rectal Surgery. Palatine, IL: American Society of Colon and Rectal Surgeons.

Coombs, R. H. *Mastering Medicine*. New York: The Free Press, 1978, 187.

Glaxo Medical Specialty Survey. Glaxo Pharmaceuticals, 1989.

Iserson, Kenneth. *Getting into a Residency*, 2nd edition. Columbia, SC: Cambden House, 1990.

Kendall, P. L. *et al.* "Medical Specialization Trends and Contributing Factors" in *Psychological Aspects of Medical Training*. Springfield, IL: Charles C. Thomas, 1971.

Mandelbaum-Schmid, J. "Emergency Medicine Is Coming of Age." *MD*, 35(8):28–36, 1991.

McCauley, M. H. *The Myers Longitudinal Medical Study*. Gainesville, FL: 1978.

"Medical Students Rate Family Over Income in Choosing a Specialty." *Physicians Financial News*, 6(1):1, 1988.

Pediatrics: What's It Really Like? The American Academy of Pediatrics, 141 Northwest Point, Elk Grove Village, IL 60009.

Rowley, B. D. *et al.* "Selected Characteristics of Graduates. Medical Education in the United States." *Journal of the American Medical Association*, 266(7):936.

Scherger, Joseph *et al.* "Responses to Questions by Medical Students about Family Practice." *The Journal of Family Practice*, 26:2:169–196.

Schwartz, R. W. *et al.* "Controllable Lifestyle, a New Factor in Career Choice for Medical Students." *Academic Medicine*, 64(10):606–609, 1989.

Taylor, Anita. *How to Choose a Medical Specialty*. Philadelphia: W. B. Saunders Co., 1993.

Voelker, R. "Prevention Tries to Break into the Medical Mainstream." *American Medical News*, 38(18):2, 79, 1992.

Wagenson, E. O. "Internist Angst." *The New Physician*, 41(2): 18–23, 1992.

Wagoner, N. E., *et al.* "Factors Used by Program Directors to Select Residents." *Journal of Medical Education*, 61(1):10–21, 1986.

What is Nuclear Medicine? Washington, DC: American College of Nuclear Physicians, 1995.

Which Medical Specialty for You? American Board of Medical Specialties. Evanston, IL: One Rotary Center, Suite 805, Evanston, IL 60201-5913, 1995.

FINANCING A MEDICAL EDUCATION

Cohn, Victor. "Medical School Debt: You and I Pay." *Washington Post*, July 21, 1992.

Federal Student Aid Fact Sheet. 1990–91. Washington, DC: Department of Education, Student Aid Information Office, P.O. Box 84, Washington, DC 20044.

Financial Planning Guide for Medical Students in the U.S. Educational and Scientific Trust of Pennsylvania Medical Society, P.O. Box 8820, 777 East Park Drive, Harrisburg, PA 17105-8820.

Financial Planning and Management Manual for U.S. Medical Students, 1994. Washington, DC: Association of American Medical Colleges, Dept. 66, Washington, DC 20055.

Financing Medical Education, 1992–1993. Boston: Boston University School of Medicine, 80 East Concord Street, Boston, MA 02118.

Financing Your Health Professions Education and Financial Planning and Debt Management for Health Professions. New York: National Medical Fellowships, Inc, 1993.

Informed Decision-Making. Part I, Financial Planning and Management for Medical Students. Part II, Sources of Financial Assistance for Medical School. New York: National Medical Fellowships, Inc.

Schlachter, G. A. *Directory of Financial Aids for Women*. 6th Edition. Reference Service Press, 1100 Industrial Road, Suite 9, San Carlos, CA 94070.

MEDICAL PRACTICE

Balk, Sophie. "Is Part-time Practice for You?" *Life in Medicine*, July 1995.

Balliott, Gene. *Getting Started in a Medical Practice*. Medical Economics Press.

Borzo, Greg. "Solo Practice: A Contrarian's View." *American Medical News*, July 24, 1995.

Buying and Selling a Medical Practice: A Valuation Guide. American Medical Association, 515 North State Street, Chicago, IL 60610.

Donahugh, Donald M. *Practice Management for Physicians*. Philadelphia: W. B. Saunders, 1986.

"Guilt: Don't Take It to Work with You." *Life in Medicine,* July 1995.

Iglehart, John K. "The Future Supply of Physicians." *New England Journal of Medicine*, 314:13:860–864.

Mitka, Mike. "HMO Stampede Celebrates Big Enrollment Gains." *American Medical News*, July 24, 1995.

Physician Characteristics and Distribution in the United States. American Medical Association Fulfillment and Distribution Center, P.O. Box 10944, Chicago, IL 60610.

Practice Affiliation: Forming or Joining a Partnership or Group. American Medical Association Fulfillment and Distribution Center, P.O. Box 10944, Chicago, IL 60610.

Socioeconomic Characteristics of Medical Practice, 1995. Chicago: American Medical Association Center for Health Policy Research, 515 North State Street, Chicago, IL 60610.

Tenery, Robert M., Jr. "Is Medicine a Profession or a Business?" *American Medical News*, December 8, 1989.

Todd, James R. *Physician's Survival Guide: Legal Pitfalls and Solutions*. Chicago: American Medical Association, 515 North State Street, Chicago, IL 60610.

Torrey, Karen. "For Some, Medicine Is the Right Choice Later in Life." *American Medical News*, July 14, 1989.

Turow, Joseph. "Hospital Healthcare Executives on TV: Image Problems for the Profession." *Hospital and Health Services Administration*, November-December 1989.

MEDICAL SCHOOL

Boodman, Sandra G. "Applications Growing for Medical Schools." (Washington Health). *The Washington Post*, May 9, 1995.

Getting In: A Guide for Pre-Med Students. Premedical Education Task Force, 1993. American Medical Student Association, 19-2 Association Drive, Reston, VA 22091.

Krieger, Gary F. "Are We Choosing the Best Students for Medical School." Vol. 37. *American Medical News*, October 3, 1994.

Leopold, Wendy. "The Medical School Charts a New Course." *Medicine on the Midway*. University of Chicago, Winter 1990–91.

Lerner, M. *Medical School: The Interview and the Applicant*. Barron's Educational Series, Inc., 250 Wireless Boulevard, Hauppague, NY 11788.

Martin, Toni. *How to Survive Medical School*. New York: Holt, Rinehart and Winston, 1983.

MCAT Programs. The American College Testing Program, 2255 North Dubuque Road, P.O. Box 414, Iowa City, IA 52243.

Medical School Admissions Requirements: United States and Canada. Washington, DC: Association of American Medical Schools, 43rd Edition, 1996–1997.

Nash, Ira S. and Richard C. Pasternak. "Physician: Educate Thyself." Vol. 273, *Journal of the American Medical Association*, May 17, 1995.

"The Number of Students Applying to U.S. Medical Schools Has Broken the All-time Record . . ." Vol. 14, *Medicine and Health*, August 30, 1993.

Sadeghi-Nejad, Ab and Marion M. Marquardt. "Medical School Applicants and the Appeal of Medicine as a Career." Vol. 93. *American Journal of Medicine*. September, 1992.

Salwen, Kevin G. "Doctors to Be Flock to Medical Schools and Find Physicians Are in Short Supply." (Association of Medical Schools). *The Wall Street Journal*, June 8, 1993.

Seligmann, Jean. "Medical Schools Prescribe More TLC." *Chicago Sun-Times*. August 13, 1991.

Slomski, Anita J. "Will Med Schools Solve the Primary-Care Shortage?" Vol. 70, *Medical Economics*, July 26, 1993.

MEDICINE AS A PROFESSION

Benjamin, Walter W. "Will Centrifugal Forces Destroy the Medical Profession?" *New England Journal of Medicine*. Vol. 321, October 26, 1989.

Dorsen, Peter. "An MD Escapes the Unspoken Agony of His Profession." *American Medical News*, Vol. 32, February 24, 1989.

"Dr. Rogers: Unity to Save Medicine as a Profession." *American Medical News*. Vol. 29, p. 2, June 27, 1986.

Eisenberg, Carla. "Medicine Is No Longer a Man's Profession." *New England Journal of Medicine*, 321:22. November 30, 1989.

Millman, Nancy. "AMA Ready to Polish Up Doctor's Image." *Chicago Sun-Times*, August 12, 1991.

Physicians' Compensation in Specialty & Production Survey, Medical Group Management Association, 1995.

Rosenbaum, Edward E. "A Taste of My Own Medicine." *Plus*, Vol. 29:50. July 1988.

MINORITIES IN MEDICINE

Career Choices: Health Professions Opportunities for Minorities. Office of Statewide Health Planning and Development, Health Professions Center Opportunity Program, 1900 Ninth Street, Sacramento, CA.

Financial Aid for Minorities in Medical Fields, 1993. Garrett Park Press, P.O. Box 190, Garrett Park, MD 20896.

Health Pathways, nineteenth edition. Health Professions Career Opportunity Program, 1600 Ninth Street, Room 441, Sacramento, CA 95814.

Huckman, Beverly B. and Bruce Rattenbury. "The Need to Bring more Minority Students into Medicine." Vol. 35, *American Medical News*, August 3, 1992.

McCormick, Bryan. "Why Are There So Few Minorities in Medicine?" Vol. 36, *American Medical News*, January 4, 1993.

Medical Minorities in Medicine: A Guide for Premedical Students. Statewide Health Planning and Development, Health Professions Career Opportunity Program, 1600 Ninth Street, Room 441, Sacramento, CA 95814.

Schlachter, G. A. and D. Weber. *Directory of Financial Aids for Minorities, 1995–96*. San Carlos, CA: Reference Service Press, 1100 Industrial Road, Suite 9, San Carlos, CA 94070.

OSTEOPATHY AS A CAREER

Fast Facts, 1995. Chicago: American Osteopathic Association, 142 East Ontario Street, Chicago, IL 60611.

1995 American Osteopathic Association Directory. Chicago: American Osteopathic Association, 142 East Ontario Street, Chicago, IL 60611.

Osteopathic Medicine: A Distinctive Branch of Mainstream Medicine. Chicago: American Osteopathic Association, 142 East Ontario Street, Chicago, IL 60611.

Osteopathic Medicine as a Career. Chicago: American Osteopathic Association, 142 East Ontario Street, Chicago, IL 60611.

What Everyone Should Know About Osteopathic Medicine. Chicago: American Osteopathic Association, 142 East Ontario Street, Chicago, IL 60611.

What Is a D.O.? What Is an M.D.? Chicago: American Osteopathic Association, 142 East Ontario Street, Chicago, IL 60611.

WOMEN IN MEDICINE

American Medical Association, Women in Medicine Services, Women in Medicine in America: In the Mainstream. Chicago: American Medical Association, 515 North State Street, Chicago, IL 60610.

Arold, R. *et al.* "Taking Care of Patients. Does It Matter Whether the Physician Is a Woman?" *Journal of Medicine*, 149:729-733, December 1988.

Association of Women Surgeons. *Pocket Mentor: A Manual for Surgical Residents*. Westmont, IL: Association of Women Surgeons, 1993.

Bickel, J. "Women in Education: A Status Report." *New England Journal of Medicine*, 319:1579–1584. December 1988.

Bickel, J. and R. Quinnie. *Building a Stronger Women's Program: Enhancing the Educational and Professional Environment*. Washington, DC: AAMC, 1993.

Grant, I. "The Gender Climate of Medical School." *Journal of the American Medical Women's Association*, 43:109–119. July-August 1988.

Kaplan, S., "Motivation for Women Over 30 Going to Medical School." *Journal of Medical Education*, 58:856–57.

Lenhart, S. and C. Evans. "Sexual Harassment of Gender Discrimination: A Primer for Women Physicians." *Journal of American Medical Womens' Association*, 46:77–82, May-June 1991.

Levinson, W. *et al.* "Women in Academic Medicine: Combining Career and Family." *New England Journal of Medicine*, 321:1511–7, 1989.

Lillemoe, K. *et al.* "Surgery—Still an Old Boys Club?" *Surgery*, 116:255–61, 1994.

Mendelsohn, K. *et al* "Sex and Gender Bias in Anatomy and Physical Diagnosis." *Journal of the American Medical Association*, 272:1267–70, 1994.

Page, L. "Will Women Become the New OB-Gyn Majority?" *American Medical News*, 34(46):10–11, 1991.

Stobo, J., *et al.* "Understanding and Eradicating Bias Against Women in Medicine." *Academic Medicine*, 68:249, 1993.

Walters, B. *et al. The Annotated Bibliography of Women in Medicine*, 1993. Toronto: Ontario Medical Association, 525 University Avenue, Suite 300, Toronto, Ontario.

Women Physicians in American Medicine. 1987. Oxford University Press.

VGM CAREER BOOKS

BUSINESS PORTRAITS
Boeing
Coca-Cola
Ford
McDonald's

CAREER DIRECTORIES
Careers Encyclopedia
Dictionary of Occupational Titles
Occupational Outlook Handbook

CAREERS FOR
Animal Lovers; Bookworms; Caring
People; Computer Buffs; Crafty
People; Culture Lovers;
Environmental Types; Fashion Plates;
Film Buffs; Foreign Language
Aficionados; Good Samaritans;
Gourmets; Health Nuts; History
Buffs; Kids at Heart; Music Lovers;
Mystery Buffs; Nature Lovers; Night
Owls; Number Crunchers; Plant
Lovers; Shutterbugs; Sports Nuts;
Travel Buffs; Writers

CAREERS IN
Accounting; Advertising; Business;
Child Care; Communications;
Computers; Education; Engineering;
the Environment; Finance;
Government; Health Care; High
Tech; Horticulture & Botany;
International Business; Journalism;
Law; Marketing; Medicine; Science;
Social & Rehabilitation Services

CAREER PLANNING
Beating Job Burnout
Beginning Entrepreneur
Big Book of Jobs
Career Planning & Development for
    College Students &
    Recent Graduates
Career Change
Career Success for People with
    Physical Disabilities
Careers Checklists
College and Career Success for Students
    with Learning Disabilities
Complete Guide to Career Etiquette
Cover Letters They Don't Forget
Dr. Job's Complete Career Guide
Executive Job Search Strategies
Guide to Basic Cover Letter Writing
Guide to Basic Résumé Writing
Guide to Internet Job Searching
Guide to Temporary Employment
Job Interviewing for College Students
Joyce Lain Kennedy's Career Book

Out of Uniform
Parent's Crash Course in Career
    Planning
Slame Dunk Résumés
Up Your Grades: Proven Strategies
    for Academic Success

CAREER PORTRAITS
Animals; Cars; Computers;
Electronics; Fashion; Firefighting;
Music; Nature; Nursing; Science;
Sports; Teaching; Travel; Writing

GREAT JOBS FOR
Business Majors
Communications Majors
Engineering Majors
English Majors
Foreign Language Majors
History Majors
Psychology Majors
Sociology Majors

HOW TO
Apply to American Colleges and
    Universities
Approach an Advertising Agency and
    Walk Away with the Job You Want
Be a Super Sitter
Bounce Back Quickly After
    Losing Your Job
Change Your Career
Choose the Right Career
Cómo escribir un currículum vitae en
    inglés que tenga éxito
Find Your New Career Upon
    Retirement
Get & Keep Your First Job
Get Hired Today
Get into the Right Business School
Get into the Right Law School
Get into the Right Medical School
Get People to Do Things Your Way
Have a Winning Job Interview
Hit the Ground Running in Your
    New Job
Hold It All Together When You've
    Lost Your Job
Improve Your Study Skills
Jumpstart a Stalled Career
Land a Better Job
Launch Your Career in TV News
Make the Right Career Moves
Market Your College Degree
Move from College into a
    Secure Job
Negotiate the Raise You Deserve
Prepare Your Curriculum Vitae

Prepare for College
Run Your Own Home Business
Succeed in Advertising When all You
Succeed in College
Succeed in High School
Take Charge of Your Child's Early
    Education
Write a Winning Résumé
Write Successful Cover Letters
Write Term Papers & Reports
Write Your College Application Essay

MADE EASY
College Applications
Cover Letters
Getting a Raise
Job Hunting
Job Interviews
Résumés

**ON THE JOB: REAL PEOPLE
    WORKING IN...**
Communications
Health Care
Sales & Marketing
Service Businesses

OPPORTUNITIES IN
This extensive series provides detailed
    information on more than 150
    individual career fields.

RÉSUMÉS FOR
Advertising Careers
Architecture and Related Careers
Banking and Financial Careers
Business Management Careers
College Students &
    Recent Graduates
Communications Careers
Computer Careers
Education Careers
Engineering Careers
Environmental Careers
Ex-Military Personnel
50+ Job Hunters
Government Careers
Health and Medical Careers
High School Graduates
High Tech Careers
Law Careers
Midcareer Job Changes
Nursing Careers
Re-Entering the Job Market
Sales and Marketing Careers
Scientific and Technical Careers
Social Service Careers
The First-Time Job Hunter

VGM Career Horizons
a division of *NTC Publishing Group*
4255 West Touhy Avenue
Lincolnwood, Illinois 60646–1975